A. E. J. (Alfred Edward John) Cavendish, H. E. (Henry Edward Pane) Goold-Adams

Korea and the Sacred White Mountain

A. E. J. (Alfred Edward John) Cavendish, H. E. (Henry Edward Pane) Goold-Adams

Korea and the Sacred White Mountain

ISBN/EAN: 9783743447967

Printed in Europe, USA, Canada, Australia, Japan

Cover: Foto ©ninafisch / pixelio.de

More available books at **www.hansebooks.com**

KOREANS IN WINTER CLOTHING, FU-SAN.

KOREA

AND THE

SACRED WHITE MOUNTAIN

BEING A BRIEF ACCOUNT OF A JOURNEY IN KOREA IN 1891

By Captain A. E. J. CAVENDISH, F.R.G.S.
1st Argyll and Sutherland Highlanders

TOGETHER WITH

AN ACCOUNT OF AN ASCENT OF THE WHITE MOUNTAIN

By Captain H. E. GOOLD-ADAMS, R.A.

WITH FORTY ORIGINAL ILLUSTRATIONS AND TWO SPECIALLY PREPARED MAPS.

LONDON
GEORGE PHILIP & SON, 32 FLEET STREET, E.C.
LIVERPOOL: 45 TO 51 SOUTH CASTLE STREET
1894

INTRODUCTION

THE following narrative of the way in which a few weeks' leave was spent in Korea in 1891, does not pretend to any literary merit or to be a detailed account of that little-known country; it is simply an amplification of my diary during that time.

It was at first intended that Captain Goold-Adams, R.A., and I should jointly publish the accounts of our journeys, but as he is still in the Far East, the collaboration had to be abandoned. However, Chapter viii. is a short narrative of his ascent of the "White Mountain," in which, for reasons given in my story, I was unable to accompany him. Unfortunately his map, and notes of his observations for position during his solitary journey, were lost by a friend to whom he lent them.

My thanks are due to Mr. C. W. Campbell, of the Chinese Consular Service, for kindly allowing me to make use of some of the photographs which he took during his journey to the "White Mountain" in 1889; also to Mr. Hillier and Mr. Brazier for their photographs.

The photograph of the lake on the summit of the "White Mountain" is combined from three views taken by Captain Goold-Adams; owing to the defective state of the films, our Kodak pictures were, with this solitary exception, total failures.

The native sketches were executed for me by a Korean gentleman, and are, I think, interesting as illustrations of the manners and customs of the country; it is to be regretted that more of the artist's colouring could not be reproduced.

We cannot express sufficiently our gratitude to the many foreign residents in Korea, Shanghai, and Chefoo, from whom we received the utmost kindness and hospitality.

We shall never regret the time spent in Korea, amidst its strange people, wild scenery, and lovely climate. The small discomforts we had to undergo are inseparable from travel in a country some three thousand years behind modern civilisation, and, in our case, these were reduced greatly by the civility of the Mandarins and officials.

A. E. J. CAVENDISH.

EDINBURGH, 1893.

KOREA

AND THE

SACRED WHITE MOUNTAIN

CHAPTER I.

HONG-KONG TO SOŬL.

ON Friday, August 28th, we reached Chémulpho, the maritime port of the capital of Korea, after a journey of thirteen days from Hong-Kong, having left that place on the 15th for Shanghai. After staying at the Shanghai Club, which is the pride of the Far East, and a luxurious haven of rest for the traveller, for four days, during which time we engaged a cook and a servant, we again embarked on the 23rd. Early morning of the 25th saw us at Chefoo, where we had to change steamers; the landing with all our goods was accomplished at 8 A.M. at a stone pier surrounded by coal-barges, on which, as on many of the junks and sampans, the coolies were working stark naked. Having been armed with a letter of introduction to Mr. Donnelly, a prominent resident, Goold-Adams and I were, by his kindness, enabled to make use of the club while boarding and sleeping at the hotel close by.

Chefoo is the watering-place for Korea, Pekin, Tientsin, and Shanghai, but the foreign portion of it is very small, with three indifferent boarding-houses, but good pears and good bathing, if you do not mind a naked fisherman or two about. The chief exports appear to be straw plait for hats and bean-cake for manure. Whilst here, we were most kindly entertained by Mr. and Mrs. Donnelly, and with them and Mr. and Mrs. Bellington, we crossed the bay to visit a fort which was built twenty-five years ago by General Snell, a German employé of the Chinese Government. No guns have ever been mounted and the fort is rapidly falling into ruins; in any case, it would be useless against artillery fire from men-of-war. A very fine view of Chefoo is to be obtained from the dilapidated officers' mess-house, which crowns the highest part of the hill on which the fort is built. Chefoo rejoices in a garrison of 500 Chinese soldiers, of whose drill and discipline I had no time to obtain any idea; but their dress and equipment, judging from a brief glimpse, is a strange medley of prehistoric and modern ideas on weapons, drill, and costume.

Bellington, who is the Superintending Engineer of the Tientsin Railway, told us some stories about the Chinese and their extraordinary ideas on the subject of railways. The track is not fenced in, and people kept crossing it to the danger of their lives ; wherefore the local mandarins said the engine must have eyes painted on it, to enable it to see where it was going. A junk has to have eyes to see its proper course ; why not a railway engine ? They were not satisfied when told that the buffers did as well, but said a man ought to be sent on ahead mounted on a donkey to warn people off the track. This might do very well for some English and European railways, but on this little line the ordinary speed is twenty-five miles an hour! Once there was a collision and a good deal of rolling stock was damaged ; the mandarins wanted to leave the débris where it was, and build a new track round the heap ; they were naturally much astonished when they found the line cleared by the next day, a work which included the lifting of two 42-ton engines.

The captain of the *Tsurugu Maru*, the steamer of the Nippon Yusen Kaisha line, which conveyed us from Chefoo to Chémulpho, Devenish by name, had been chief officer of the steamer when it rescued some Chinese sailors from drowning. It seems that these men (thirteen, I think) were capsized in their junk while on their way from Chefoo to Chémulpho, and when found, had been clinging to the bottom of their craft for eight days ; when brought on board the steamer, the instant the first man stepped on its deck, he snatched a pipe from one of the Chinese passengers and took a couple of hearty puffs from it. He and his companions all recovered from their exposure and were sent back to Chefoo. In addition to their junk, they lost 200 dollars, which were in a locker in the hold, and could not be got at. In recognition of his services and kindness, the Guild of traders to which they belonged presented Devenish with a square scarlet tablet, on which were set forth in gold letters the story of the rescue and their appreciation of his humanity.

CHÉMULPHO AT LOW TIDE, FROM NORTH-WEST.

It was high tide at Chémulpho when we landed to pay our respects to Mr. Kerr, the British Vice-Consul, and we got ashore without difficulty. It being exceedingly hot (88°), and hearing that a Japanese steam-launch would be going to Soŭl next day, we decided not to go by land, a distance of twenty-seven miles, although the road is good except in wet weather, but to trust ourselves and our baggage in the

CONTENTS

		PAGE
INTRODUCTION		5

CHAP.
I.	HONG-KONG TO SOŬL	11
II.	SOŬL	23
III.	SOŬL TO WON-SAN	50
IV.	WON-SAN	85
V.	WON-SAN TO CHANG-JIN	101
VI.	CHANG-JIN TO KAP-SAN	131
VII.	KAP-SAN TO PO-CHÖN	144
VIII.	THE ASCENT OF THE "WHITE MOUNTAIN"	158
IX.	PO-CHÖN TO WON-SAN	182
X.	ON SPORT IN KOREA	202
	ITINERARY	209
	INDEX	215

ILLUSTRATIONS

NATIVE SKETCHES ILLUSTRATING MANNERS AND CUSTOMS.

I. JUDICIAL EXAMINATION UNDER TORTURE	. To face page	24
II. STARCHING AND IRONING .	,, ,,	26
III. SPINNING FLAX . . .	,, ,,	40
IV. POST-MORTEM EXAMINATION IN SUSPECTED CASE . .	,, ,,	46
V. WEAVING CLOTH. (*In colours*) .	between pages 52 and	53
VI. A BLACKSMITH . . .	. to face page	54
VII. TIGHT-ROPE DANCING	,, ,,	62
VIII. THRESHING GRAIN . .	,, ,,	70
IX. DANCING GIRLS AND MUSICIANS	,, ,,	80
X. PLOUGHING AND SOWING	,, ,,	84
XI. A HAT-BAND MAKER	,, ,,	92
XII. A HAT MAKER	,, ,,	94
XIII. AN OFFICIAL ON A JOURNEY. (*In colours*)	. between pages 114 and	115
XIV. BRIDEGROOM GOING TO BRIDE'S HOUSE. (*In colours*) ,,	132 ,,	133
XV. BRIDEGROOM PLEDGING BRIDE IN WEDDING-CUP ,, ,,	134 ,,	135
XVI. BOYS AT SCHOOL. (*In colours*) . .	,, 142 ,,	143
XVII. A HAWKING PARTY	. . to face page	146
XVIII. PLAYING A COMEDY. (*In colours*) .	. between pages 180 and	181
XIX. A HIGH-CLASS FUNERAL. (*In colours*) .	,, 192 ,,	193
XX. SERVICE OF THE BUDDHIST PRIESTS	. to face page	200

LIST OF ILLUSTRATIONS

NARRATIVE ILLUSTRATIONS.

1. Koreans in winter clothing, Fu-san	*Photo*		*Frontispiece*
2. Chémulpho at low-tide from north-west	*Photo*—Mr. C. W. CAMPBELL		page 14
3. Soŭl, looking south	„ —Mr. HILLIER		„ 23
4. Rough sketch of coolie pack-frame			„ 35
5. Ready to start	*Photo*—Mr. HILLIER		„ 50
6. Rough sketch of water-mill			„ 75
7. Prefectural Yamen at Won-san	*Photo*—Mr. BRAZIER		„ 87
8. Won-san, looking east-north-east	„	*to face*	„ 88
9. A tiger-trap	„ „		„ 98
10. Rough sketch of native cart			„ 111
11. Rough sketch of bridge at Teuk-sil-töng			„ 124
12. Settler's hut near Un-chong	*Photo*—Mr. CAMPBELL		„ 149
13. Hunter and guides, Po-chŏn	„		„ 151
14. Distant View of Paik-tu-san or White Mountain	*Sketch*—Captain CAVENDISH	*to face*	„ 152
15. The Amnok or Yalu, near the "White Mountain"	*Photo*—Mr. CAMPBELL		„ 159
16. Korean bearers	„ „		„ 168
17. Chinese hunter's lodge	„ „		„ 171
18. The lake on the "White Mountain"	„ —Capt. GOOLD-ADAMS		„ 174
19. Puk-chong, looking south-west	*Photo*—Mr. CAMPBELL		„ 190
20. Ham-heung Bridge, looking south-east	„ „		„ 197

MAPS.

1. Map of Korea	*to face page*	11
2. Map of Part of Korea, showing the Author's Route	„ „	214

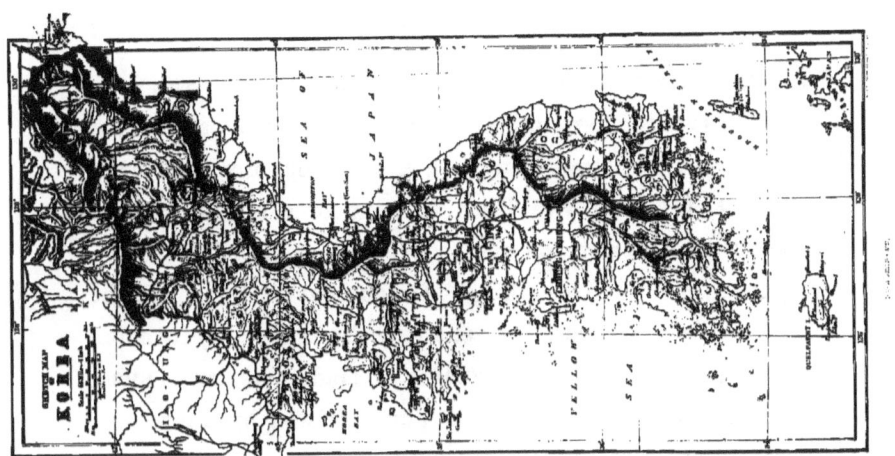

Japanese craft, in spite of sinister rumours concerning its habit of running aground, &c. Accordingly we transferred our baggage to the steam-launch, a thing about fifty feet long, and after lunching with Kerr, we went for a walk round the place with Devenish, on the chance of getting a little snipe-shooting, but we saw nothing. On our way back through the native village, we were overtaken by the Prefect of Inchhön, who is the Korean Superintendent of Trade here, borne along in a box-like chair, preceded and followed by attendants, some armed with pikes, some with trumpets, and some with fans. A respectful demeanour is required from the bystanders when the great man passes by, and we were amused to see one of his "soldiers," every now and then, rush at a man who had not left off smoking, seize his pipe, break it in pieces and throw them away, at the same time whacking the smoker over the head with his fan. After dining with Kerr and Laporte, who is the assistant Customs officer here, we passed the night at Steward's Hotel.; Steward being a Chinaman, who had been a steward on a ship, hence the name he adopted for his hotel and store here and at Soŭl. The hotel was primitive in its ways and the beds were mighty hard, but we were most agreeably surprised to find anything of the kind and so clean and comfortable in the place. Inchhön is the name of the prefecture, of the second class, whose magistrate resides five miles from Chémulpho, while the Chinese name for the latter place is Jenchuan, and the Japanese is Jinsen.

Next morning at 7 A.M. we succeeded in getting on board the steam-launch, which, however, did not start till an hour later, and this delay was the cause of our subsequent troubles, by making us miss the tide. Chémulpho at low water presents a remarkable sight, for owing to the rise and fall of the tide being thirty-six feet, very little water remains in the harbour, only a narrow channel in the middle, just wide enough for a steamer to swing in, while the rest of the harbour becomes a vast expanse of mud flat, only broken in one place by a small rocky island.

It was hot enough to-day (87°) for the coolies belonging to the junks and sampans, both Korean and Japanese, to work stark naked, as at Chefoo. Whilst waiting on board the launch we saw the late Russian Envoy to Korea, M. Waeber, getting himself and his baggage on board the *Tsurugu Maru, en route* back to Russia. Under his auspices a very fine embassy has been erected in a good situation in Soŭl, compared with which the new British Consulate-General in the capital is remarkably hideous. Our fellow-passengers consisted of "Brother" Jones, a young American missionary, who had come with us from Chefoo; Steinbeck, a German, who kept a store in Chémulpho; his servant; about fifty Japanese men and women, and a few Chinese and Koreans; one of the latter smoked and expectorated incessantly. This custom is, to an Englishman, one of the most annoying habits of the Koreans; the Chinese are bad enough in this way, but they apparently do not spit unless they really have an obstruction in the throat, but Koreans, after clearing their throats with a great deal of disgusting noise, produce nine times out of ten nothing at all. I timed this particular gentleman, and found he cleared his throat on an average six times in five minutes during the whole time we enjoyed his company on the launch, which, I fancy, equals the performances of any Scotch loafer! Soon after eight we started, and steamed slowly along the coast and up the river Han with the tide, the influence of which is felt a long way past the capital. The shifting bed of the river, its shallowness, numerous sandbanks, and strong current at ebb-tide render its navigation very difficult. Low rocky hills, gradually merging into barren, brown, and dreary mountains, enclosed the valley of the river, here from 100 to 300 yards wide; every two or three miles, on either bank, a stone wall, three or four feet high, ran from the water's edge to the top of the hill, as a protection against invasion, while on every eminence was a small stone fort, which, like the walls, was in ruins; a dilapidated wall also ran along the right bank of the river, broken here and there by small villages or ferry stations; these fortifications were erected after the Japanese invasion of 1592. At noon we grounded on a sandbank, remaining fast for fifteen minutes, but after much going astern of the engine, we managed to get off and go ahead once more. However, at 3.30, by which time the tide was on the ebb, we grounded once more, and nothing would move us. The Japanese in charge of the launch, seeing some Koreans in a small boat towing a junk down-stream, put off in their skiff and seized the boat, not without a lengthy altercation with the owners and some blows with a bamboo. Returning in triumph, they made some of our Korean passengers get into the boat, with the object of lightening the launch, but she had so much cargo on board that this was in vain. After some time they told us we should have to stop there for the night, and as there was no accommodation of any kind and we wanted our dinner, we prevailed on a Korean junk, which was gaily sailing up the river, to take us on board; but no sooner had we boarded her, than the owners said the current was too strong and they must anchor. We would not allow this, and took charge of the junk; but we were not enough to hoist and work the huge unwieldy sail and likewise steer, so we put the master of the junk to do the latter while we did the former. By "we," I mean Goold-Adams, "Brother Jones," Steinbeck, myself, Steinbeck's boy, and three Koreans; the rest of the crew sulked and did nothing. However, after the steersman had twice purposely let her fall away, we gave up and drifted down to the launch, getting on board her again with some difficulty. Very shortly after this, two naked Japs on board a Japanese junk agreed to take us to Mapuh, the river port of Soŭl, and we (as before) transferred ourselves to their craft. We sailed merrily along until 6.30 P.M., when the wind died away, and the current being too strong to row, or rather "ulo" against, we had to anchor for the night about five miles short of our destination. Goold-Adams and I were tolerably hungry, as all we had had during the day was an egg for breakfast, and some sandwiches and a bottle of beer for luncheon. Fortunately Steinbeck had some bread, claret, and brandy left in his basket, and he kindly shared what he had amongst the four of us. The Japanese were very civil, made us some tea, spread mats on the deck of the junk for us to lie on, and stretched the sail over the boom to form an awning to keep off the dew. We were very uncomfortable, however, and although the junk was as clean as it could be, yet, as the cargo consisted of matches, dried fish, and cabbage, the smell was awful. One of the Koreans transferred himself to a Korean junk, which anchored alongside us, and the two others slept in their white cotton clothes on the roof of the junk; they presented next morning a miserable spectacle of wet, blue, and shivering humanity! We had each brought a bag with us, leaving the other things on the launch with the servants, so we were able to make some sort of pillow for ourselves, but we slept very little; that smell was too much!

Rousing ourselves at 4 A.M. on Sunday morning, we found a dense fog hanging over the river, and had great difficulty in getting the Japs to start before daylight; at last we got off, but after they had "uloed" for half-an-hour, they swore they were going down-stream. However, by dint of much explanation through Steinbeck's cook, who could speak some Japanese, we persuaded them that, as long as the bow pointed S.E. according to their compass, we must be going right, and that we had not again passed a cliff near which we had anchored for the night. We stopped once or twice and let down the anchor, while we inquired of a passing Korean junk or sent the boat ashore to ask at a house where Soŭl was; but the Koreans all lied, some saying it was in one direction, others in a totally different one.

The day was now breaking, and the Japs recognising the shore, finally landed us at Hang-pai-do, a ferry about two miles from the regular landing-place, Mapuh, at 6.30 A.M.; we each paid the boatmen one dollar for their trouble and civility, except the Koreans, who, *more suo*, each paid nothing, and after getting some men to carry our bags, we walked the six miles into Soŭl through a most fertile country, along a road which was now decent, but in wet weather must be impassable mud in places. In every valley grew castor-oil plants, rice, beans, maize, chillies, millet, tobacco, "su-su," &c., right up to the suburbs of the capital. We entered Soŭl by the west gate, an erection about forty feet high, with the usual curled roof of tiles and official painted ornamentation; the wooden gates were about twelve feet high, and studded with iron nails, while the wall itself was about twenty feet high and twelve feet thick. Through terribly smelling lanes, Goold-Adams and I were kindly piloted by "Brother Jones" to the gate of the house, where Mr. Hillier, the Consul-General, was temporarily living while the new Consulate-General was being built, and we thankfully got to a comfortable dwelling at 8.30 A.M. Mr. Hillier was at church, but turned up in time for breakfast, giving us a hearty welcome. After our toilette he took us to the Consular office, where we were introduced to Mr. Scott, the Vice-Consul, an ardent Korean scholar, and author of a vocabulary and dictionary in that language. Afterwards we called on Mr. Schoenicke, head of the Korean Customs department, and also on the Italian Consul, where we met Lieutenant-Colonel Nienstead, the instructor of the Korean army.

The Colonel arrived in Korea in 1889 as a captain, in 1890 he was made a major, and in 1891 he became lieutenant-colonel; he told us some amusing facts about the Korean army, but naturally made the best of it. Mr. Hillier most kindly insisted on our staying with him while we remained in Soŭl, and with Mr. Scott busied himself in getting an interpreter and ponies for our journey to Won-san; he also sent a "soldier" to show us round the town, but as the man could not speak anything but Korean, we were not so much struck with things as we might otherwise have been.

The streets were narrow and tortuous; on each side was a gutter, into which the refuse and sewerage of the houses was put; some of the cross lanes did not possess a gutter, in which case the roadway was the receptacle of every species of filth. The street leading up to the King's palace, however, was sixty yards broad, bordered by the barracks of the garrison, while the approach to the lofty entrance gate was a flagged terrace thirty yards long and twenty wide, at the outer edge of which visitors to the palace had to dismount from chairs or ponies, and thence enter on foot. Near here is the great bell, by which the hours of restriction, curfew, &c., have been regulated since 1468 A.D.; at 6 P.M. the gates of the city are shut, and cannot be opened again until dawn the following morning, and after 8 P.M. no Korean man may be abroad under pain of being arrested by the patrols and flogged.

CHAPTER II.

SOŬL.

SoŭL, pronounced Sowl by foreigners, but So-ŭl by the natives, is the capital of the country and of the province of Kyŏng-

SOŬL, LOOKING SOUTH.

kwi, and it is also called Han-yang, from the river Han close by. It has over 30,000 houses, with a population of about 250,000, and covers, within its walls, an area of ten square miles. It is as much the heart of Korea, or rather more so, as Paris is the heart of France. It is the object of every Korean gentleman to live in the capital, for there every pleasure and vice is more easy of attainment, the chances of getting favourite posts by judicious flattering and canvassing of superiors are multiplied, while the finest and best of the native and foreign produce is to be procured. There is to be found the fountain-head of official corruption and "squeezing," for every member of the well-born class spends his time in seeking his share of the loaves and fishes of dishonesty (in a European sense); there lives the King, the Lord of the 10,000 islands, the Son of heaven, the Father of his people; and the sun of royalty is felt to vivify and illumine each inhabitant of Soül, be he ever so humble. The contempt shown for provincial life by all officials and every Soül-born man is most amusing, and many were the lamentations we subsequently heard from town-bred men, obliged to live elsewhere, over their sad and uninteresting existences. The acceptance of office in the provinces is merely a means to an end—that is, the amassing of wealth which may be spent in the pleasures of this life in the capital of Korea. The darkest side of the picture lies in the crowded collection of hovels, swarming with human (and insect) life, absolutely devoid of even elementary sanitation; where the use of soap and water is confined to a few of the highest classes; where

서재에 다녀오는 길

disease and vice have lived in close partnership for several hundred years; where dishonesty and oppression are carried to their utmost limits; where torture and cruelty exercise full sway, and where private and political-intrigue hampers and hinders any improvement in, or amelioration of, the conditions of life of the great bulk of the community. But the King is father of his people, and as such, the persons and property of his subjects are absolutely at the mercy of his parental will. Fortunately or unfortunately, the constitutional weakness of mind and body, inherited from a long line of debauchees, makes the King a mere puppet in the hands of his Queen, a strong-minded woman, whose relatives and adherents fill almost every appointment. The Queen only tolerates one wife—that is, herself—and should she detect His Majesty intriguing with any of the palace ladies, the wretched female is promptly degraded and despatched to some remote district, or else succumbs to some *rapid and mysterious illness!*

The revenues of the country go into the royal treasury, and are undoubtedly, in a great measure, spent in ministering to the luxuries and caprices of an absolute monarch. Since the officers of the Chinese Customs have administered the trade duties, the King's income has been vastly increased, but no material improvement in the condition of the people or country has resulted. The net revenue from customs in 1890 was over 500,000 dollars, but how much of this was spent in improving the country? As examples of the King's extravagance and of the universal corruption, the following tales will serve. Some time ago the King imported, at great expense, a small steam-launch for use on the lake in the palace-grounds, which is nearly 100 yards in diameter; he used it once, but did not like it, and it lies there still, rotting in the water. Forced somewhat to keep pace with modern ideas, the King started a Royal Hospital, and when a foreign physician visited it, he found that although not a single patient had been admitted during the nine months it had been open, yet thirty-two "Choosahs" (secretaries) and thirty servants, with all their families, were living on the premises! Also, in the progressive mood, a Royal College was started, and a foreigner was obtained to teach in it; but after he had been there two years, he was told he was no longer wanted, as native teachers now knew enough to do without him. Then came the problem, what was to be done with the deposed pedagogue? It was solved thus-wise: the Government kept him on for three years at double salary but with no duties!

An American hospital here was presided over, during the temporary absence of the physician in charge, by Dr. Wylde, who was formerly in the English Army Medical Department, and is voluntarily devoting his life and skill and fortune in ministering to the many medical needs of an ignorant, dis-

trustful, and suffering race. One of the difficulties he has to contend with is the aversion his patients have to ablution: a Korean is said to be washed only twice in his life, once when he is born, and once when he is dead; but I have, however, seen both children and adults bathing in the rivers. Amongst the crowded inhabitants of Soŭl immorality of all kinds is rampant, and as a consequence the general condition is syphilitic. Small-pox carries off great numbers every year, and infant mortality from it is very high, though innoculation is practised, as in China.

Although Koreans do not wash their bodies much, yet they are very particular about their clothing being clean, reversing the Japanese system of keeping the body clean however dirty the clothing may be. The white garments of a Korean are most carefully washed, and are beaten with wooden rollers and boards until a fine glaze is obtained. The chief sources of expense to a man lie in his clothes and his pipe; the ordinary common black hat costs three or four dollars, while a mandarin's may cost over twenty, also the constant washing and beating of the cotton clothes soon wears them out. A Korean is hardly ever seen without his long-stemmed pipe, the head of which is often of jade, though generally of brass, and the quantity of tobacco he gets through in the year must be enormous.

In spite of the heat (87°), we got our baggage up from

Mapuh by 9 A.M., and did a little business. Mr. Hillier had obtained for us a "Toonsah" or interpreter, who was supposed by some to be a Korean, and by others to be a Chinaman; the truth probably being that some of the Chinese soldiers had adopted him when a child, and taken him to China, where he learnt the language. I believe he was employed by Mr. Yüan, the Chinese Resident, to hunt down evil-doing Chinamen in Korea, and he affected the Chinese dress, the pig-tail, and shaven forehead. He could not speak or understand English, but proved himself to be a most willing and useful attendant. The two Chinese servants we had brought from Shanghai were perfectly useless, and professed to be in fear of their lives; wherefore we decided to send them back there under escort of Mr. Scott, who was proceeding to England, and engage others. Steinbeck's boy came to see us in the afternoon, and as we had seen how useful he was during our passage from Chémulpho to Soŭl, we engaged him as cook. Besides having a good character in that capacity, he could speak a certain amount of English, Korean, and Japanese. He had to go to Chémulpho to get his clothes from Steinbeck's house there, and promised faithfully to be back by September 2nd, on which day we hoped to be able to start, if the rain, which might come on at any time, did not last long; but in this we were doomed to disappointment, for next day it came on wet at one o'clock, and we were weather-bound until the 5th. The cook, having been detained by the elements, caused us some uneasiness, but turned up in the evening of the 4th with his belongings; the latter comprised a large canvas kit-bag with "W. R. Carles" painted on it, a large box, a large bundle of rugs, an umbrella, a Japanese sword, a pair of winter boots (something like half-Wellingtons), and a battered old straw hat, which we thought an excessive amount for one boy, but its weight increased afterwards. To-night after dinner, which we had in the open air in spite of the mosquitoes, came in Mr. Stripling, who has had a somewhat chequered career, and is now living on a small salary, irregularly paid by the King, as a prospector for gold and other minerals. Hearing we were in want of a servant, he very kindly offered us his own boy, a Korean, who had travelled with him a great deal in the interior, and could speak a fair amount of English. What his complete name was I have forgotten, but he answered to that of Yeung, one of the four family names in Korea, and looked about twenty-five years old; eventually we engaged him as servant and interpreter, and he turned out most useful and willing, though not over-scrupulous in some ways.

Thanks to the good offices of Mr. Hillier, we were supplied by the Minister for Foreign Affairs (Prince Ming-yuen-shao) with a letter authorising us to travel in the country, and calling on all officials to supply us with ponies, accommodation, food, money, and servants whenever we demanded them. We had brought letters to Ming-yuen-shao from his exiled brother in Hong-Kong, Ming-yuen-ik, and he acknowledged these by sending his card to us. We also obtained here our passports for Manchuria, which the Consuls, both at Tientsin and Newchwang, had sent; huge documents they were, and, as it turned out, we never required them. We had our visiting-cards printed, or rather painted, in Chinese characters on red paper. Goold-Adams' name came out all right "Goot-a-dam," but mine as "Ka-fan-di-issl" had one character too many, three being the correct number; another mistake was made in the size of the characters, which were too small, thereby detracting from our rank and dignity.

On Monday morning we visited the new Consulate-General, designed with the usual want of taste shown in British official edifices in the Far East. The Consul-General's house stands on the top of a slight eminence, and is comfortable inside as far as the size and arrangement of rooms go; the offices are a little farther down the slope, separated from the house by a terrace and lawn-tennis ground. Mr. Hillier, who is an enthusiastic botanist, had many lovely plants and flowers in a small greenhouse, and had laid out the ground already available with much taste and care; his fruit-trees were promising well, and the previous season he had had a large crop of strawberries. The original Consular buildings, a cluster of Korean houses, were to be pulled down when the new ones were finished and their sites turned into garden. Next to the Consular compound was a large garden with some fine pine-trees in it, which was the property of the Queen, but nothing would induce her to part with it to the British Government. The Koreans are great lovers of nature and admirers of scenery, and are also great pedestrians; they—that is, the men, who always seem to have plenty of time to kill—often make pilgrimages to places whence a fine view may be obtained. In the Diamond Mountains on the east coast there are eight celebrated views, to which the most high-sounding names have been given, and annually they are visited by hundreds of Koreans.

We waited about at the Consulate for two and a half hours for the owner of the ponies, from whom we wished to hire some. When he did come, he asked such an exorbitant rate that he was promptly sent away, Mr. Hillier telling "Mr. Kim," his interpreter, to see if he could not knock down the price a little. His services were not called on in vain, for next day he managed to procure ten ponies to take us and our baggage to Won-san for thirty-four dollars, and one dollar as a present if we were satisfied with the behaviour of the "mapus" or pony-attendants. With this offer we closed, and spent the day in overhauling our kit and pitching the tent to show the Toonsah how it should be done. The tent was a single one, with an upright at each door, and a jointed ridge-pole; closed at each end by a laced door, its interior dimensions were 12½ feet long by 7½ feet wide; the ridge-pole was 8 feet from the ground, and the perpendicular sides were 3½ feet in height; the weight of the whole was 75 lbs. The foreign community at Soŭl were horror-stricken at the idea of our sleeping in a tent, and told us a tiger would come and fetch us out some night; but we decided to inhabit it until the weather became too cold, and exceedingly useful and comfortable we afterwards found it. Having got over the delay about the ponies, we were still kept prisoners by the rain, but we utilised the time in repacking some of our boxes, and thereby were able to save one package; nevertheless we still had a good number, viz., camp-beds 2, tent 1, bundle of tent-poles 1, cases of whisky 3, cartridge magazines 3, box of biscuit 1, provision boxes 3, ditto with hinged lids for daily use 2, gun-cases 3, Winchester rifles 2, despatch-box 1, dressing-bag 1, canteen 1, medicine-chest 1, folding chairs 2, bedding valise 1, waterproof bags for clothes 3, roll of waterproof sheets and blankets 1, Kodak 1; total 33.

On Friday morning it was still showery, but we were able to get the ponies up for inspection and selection of our riding animals. Goold-Adams picked out a biggish grey mare, and I took the only one remaining which had not a frightful sore-back. The ponies are very small, varying from 10½ to 13 hands, generally 11½ to 12 hands, are of all shapes and colours, bad tempered and very indifferent hacks, accustomed to carry packs weighing from 200 lbs. in easy country to 120 lbs. in difficult parts; their pace is a slow walk of two to two and a half miles an hour, unless driven on, when they can do three to four miles an hour on a fairly good road. Of trotting or cantering they have only rudimentary notions, but they are as surefooted as goats or cats, and get their loads safely over the most terrible places, and round dangerous corners in a manner perfectly marvellous. The constant ascent and descent of hills tends to make the loads slip about, and horrible galls are common, but unless it is a very bad one indeed, a Korean does not take his pony out of work for a mere gall; in other respects they are kindly treated by their masters. The ponies are never gelded, and no care is taken about breeding, but every now and then one comes across a well-shaped animal. A riding-pony can do a sort of shuffle of four to five miles an hour, but this pace is only used by riders of inferior station, for in the case of an official of high rank, etiquette requires that his steed should be led, and, on great occasions, that an attendant on either side should support the great man's knee; of this we saw an instance when we were looking at the King's palace.

The forage ration consists of about 2 lbs. of beans and millet boiled in water, and the whole poured out hot into a trough; the average feed is two gallons of this mixture, given three times a day, and supplemented by 2 lbs. of chopped straw (rice or millet). Ponies are not allowed water at other times, nor do they seem to wish for it. I do not believe they are ever used for draught purposes, and the average price for a good pony is about £5 or 20,000 cash.

Other means of transport are found in donkeys, cattle, and coolies. I have seen donkeys (which are from 10 to 11 hands high, and are also used for pack and draught purposes) cantering along at a good pace, ridden by a stalwart Korean, sitting in a huge wooden saddle, which, with its trappings, left little but the animal's tail and ears to be seen. Bulls, and occasionally cows, are used as pack and draught animals; they are of large size, 13 to 14½ hands high in the south, and 12 to 13 in the north. Some are very handsome beasts, of a short-horned breed, but inclined to fall away in the hind-quarters. Their load varies from 150 lbs. in the mountains to 250 or 300 lbs. on the plains. Their pace is about two miles an hour, but as time is of no value to a Korean, this is quite fast enough for him; and we often met a native peacefully journeying from place to place, either following behind, or perched on the back of a bull, quite contented with a day's march of twelve miles. Cattle are also used for bringing in the harvest or firewood from the mountains, harnessed to rough carts or sleds; the price of a bull is about £2, 15s., or 10,000 cash, but two years ago a murrain broke out amongst the cattle, and thousands died, which has brought the price up. The Koreans are a beef-eating people, and in addition export cattle to Japan and Siberia (Wladivostock taking annually 10,000 head), besides hides, horns, and bones for manure. In 1890, the year of the murrain, 615 tons of cow-hides, valued at $147,463, and 660 tons of cow-bones, valued at $6681, were exported.

A great deal of trade-goods is carried on the backs of coolies, on a wooden frame shaped as in the sketch below.

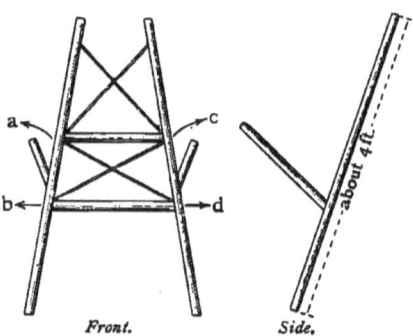

COOLIE PACK FRAME.

Braces of rope or hide pass from b and d under the armpits and over the shoulders to a and c, this is for lighter loads; for carrying heavy weights the brace passes from b over the chest to c, and another one from d to a; if the load be a high one, such as sheaves or a pile of earthenware pots, a band passes above a and c round the forehead of the coolie. A forked stick is carried in the hand, and being placed under the cross-piece, *b d*, behind, takes off some of the weight from him when the bearer desires to rest; should the bearer wish to take off his load altogether, he stoops till the legs of the frame touch the ground, then slips out of the braces, and placing the forked stick beneath the cross-piece, *b d*, behind, the load remains supported on a sort of tripod.

Trained to it from infancy, coolies can carry the most astounding loads. I was told, on good authority, they have been known to carry a load of copper ingots weighing 460 lbs. for several days together and considerable distances; but as far as I could judge, the load seems to vary from 100 lbs. in bad country to 250 lbs. on the flat. An average day's journey for a coolie, not heavily laden, is from eight to twelve miles, for cattle ten to fifteen, and for ponies twenty to twenty-five miles. A Korean when carrying a small load, such as a small bag, slings it on his back, so that the weight shall come on the loins as much as possible; he is a great walker, and can travel 100 li (or thirty-three miles) a day for weeks together without undue effort. A courier once went on foot from Won-san on the east coast to Soŭl in the winter, a distance of 175 miles, in ninety-six hours.

While in Soŭl we made acquaintance with the Italian Consul, a most ardent sportsman and photographer, and a most agreeable companion, also Dr. Wylde, whom I have mentioned above, and Mr. Trollope, a nephew of the novelist, who had left a curacy in Norfolk to follow the fortunes of Dr. Corfe, the English Missionary Bishop of Korea, and, while admiring his disinterested devotion to the good cause, we sincerely pitied him for the life he had marked out for himself, a well-educated man of the world and a thorough sportsman. I saw Colonel Nienstead several times, and talked to him about the Korean army, but his natural enthusiasm for his profession no doubt carried him on to make the very most of very little.

Strictly speaking, Korea has no army : she does not want one, nor has she pecuniary resources wherewith to provide one in a modern and Western sense. For centuries a bone of contention between China and Japan, Korea finds her safety in the jealousy between these two countries. Though conquered by the former, and now nominally her vassal, she is practically independent as far as her internal affairs are concerned; the Japanese have long coveted the country, and indeed, after several invasions, held it tributary for many years, but Korea, with the aid of China, long since emancipated herself from that yoke. Both her neighbours are eagerly competing for the lion's share in the direction of her affairs, for while the work of collecting the Customs duties at the treaty ports is administered by officers of the Chinese Customs service, the postal and banking arrangements, which are almost entirely for the benefit of the foreign section of the community, are controlled by the Japanese. The continuance of Korea as a kingdom depends, not on her military or naval resources, but on her geographical position and the jealousy of her neighbours. Any real danger there may be lies in the proximity of Russia, but even here her safety is assured by the necessity for Japan and China to unite against the annexation by Russia of a country so situated as, in the hands of a hostile power, to command their main trade routes. Moreover, other Powers would not regard with equanimity her acquisition by Russia, for it would be a standing menace to their trade, and the safety of their colonies and possessions in Eastern waters. At present the harbour of Wladivostock is closed by ice for four or five months of the year, the Trans-Siberian railway is by no means near its completion, and it will be some years before Russia, if she ever means aggression to the South, with the object of obtaining a better outlet on the Pacific, such as Won-san, will find herself strong enough in the Southern Ussuri region to take the field against Korea and her probable protectors.

With regard to the Trans-Siberian railway, although the Czarewich opened a section of it with great *éclat* in 1891, even the portion laid for the ceremony will have to be remade. Soldiers and convicts are set to work on sections of line, and about a verst's length of roadway has been made in a few places; but there appears to be no competent engineer in charge of their labour, and much of the cutting and filling will have to be done over again when the construction of the railway is seriously undertaken. As an example of how the work is carried out, I was told that a Russian contractor for part of the line, hired 800 men from Odessa, and sent them out to Wladivostock, but neither went there himself nor sent money to pay their wages; the agent there put them to work on the railway, by way of recouping himself for his preliminary expenses, but they refused to work without wages; as they had no money wherewith to return to Russia, and the agent had no money wherewith to pay their wages, they have to remain living at the expense of the inhabitants of Wladivostock.

With these assurances of freedom from molestation, Korea has no pressing need of a regular army; she has, indeed, as a nucleus, some troops trained to a certain extent with firearms by foreign officers, but these are, for the greater part, simply appanages of state. There is, moreover, a theoretical military system, based on compulsory service, by means of which it might be possible, under proper guidance, to expand this nucleus into a large army; but as a matter of practice, the service of any Korean officer or soldier is purely voluntary and limited by the dictates of his own sweet will.

The population of Korea, which is steadily though slowly

increasing, is about 14,000,000, and of this number about 1,000,000 are considered to be fighting men. For official purposes the population is reckoned by families, and on the number of families in a district the revenue due from cultivators and occupiers of land is assessed; also, following the Chinese system, every family occupying a house, or in the poorest districts every two families, has to supply, when called on, one able-bodied man for military service. Of the numbers put down as fit for fighting, not a hundredth part ever perform any duties of their military calling.

Each official has according to his rank (there are 8 Governors of provinces and 332 Prefects) a certain number of attendants, such as secretaries, seal-bearers, and "soldiers," and he increases the numbers of his retinue in proportion to his wealth. But the business of the majority of these soldiers is not fighting, but rather that of police, messengers, tax gatherers, &c.; in short, the outward symbols of the rank and importance of the individual from whom they receive, or should receive, pay. The fact of being a "soldier" confers a certain distinction on a man, and gives him considerable advantages. In the first place, he has achieved, in a lowly way, that which is the ambition of every Korean, viz., an official position; and in the second place, by virtue of this official position he has opportunities of effecting "squeezes," that is to say, the levying of black-mail, the receiving of

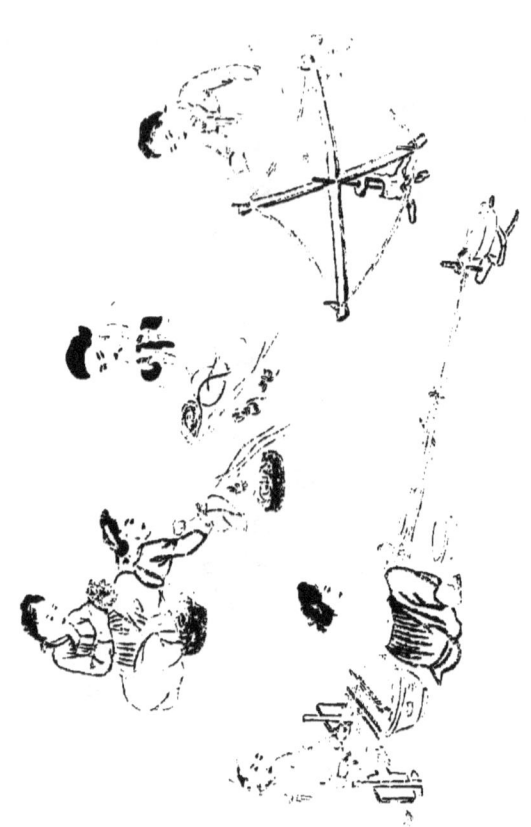

bribes from persons having business with his master, the right to travel on his master's business, and frequently on his own, at the expense of the public, and general pickings of all kinds, which are denied to the vulgar herd. It is the object in life of every one to be enabled to live a life of comparative ease at the expense of his fellow-countrymen, and it is no exaggeration to say that 20 per cent. of the whole population are idlers, supported by the labours of the remainder; hence in a great measure the poverty of the country. With this object hundreds of youths journey annually to the capital to compete at the public examinations, the passing of these as a test of merit being a *sine quâ non* for the aspirant to preferment. The final test is, I am told, the composition of a poem on a set theme from the Chinese classics, and the King is the judge; all the compositions are at a fixed time thrown into a heap, and His Majesty is supposed to select the writers of the best odes as successful candidates. However, the candidate who pays best, or has most interest, is generally selected! He has then to flatter and fawn on his superiors till he gets some minor office, whence, if he be discreet, and a relative or adherent of the party in chief power, he may rise to important and lucrative posts.

According to the military scheme, the affairs of the army are conducted by the "Board of War" or "Bing," one of the six Departments of State, consisting of a President, a Vice-

President, and a Secretary; these three are members of the General Council of the King, but the practical work of administering the army is under three other chief officers. Each province has by tradition its army, commander-in-chief, and a fleet; the capital having an army and two fleets. Naval affairs are nominally administered by Admirals, Right, Left, and Centre, under the President of the Board of War; the Korean fleets at present are non-existent, even to war-junks, beyond two small transports of 800 tons called the *Hairiong* and *Chi-riong*, which are used to bring produce down to the treaty ports from unopened ports in the north; the Government hopes, however, to procure a stern-wheel steamer, drawing two feet of water, and steaming twelve knots an hour, for protective service on the Lower Han river. As there is no army to speak of, all the above offices are in abeyance or mere sinecures.

A number of real "fighting" soldiers are kept up as guards to the King and governors of provinces; such is the garrison of Soŭl and the "army of Phyŏng-yang." The latter is from 1200 to 1500 strong, composed of reliable men of good physique, trained to fight after the native fashion with sword and gun, and part of it is invariably brought to the capital in case of any national danger. In Soŭl alone is any training, according to modern and Western military methods, performed; in other places such "soldiers" as are intended to do any fighting are trained to shoot with bows and arrows, and up to 120 yards they are for the most part very good archers. Nearly every prefectural town has its archery ground, on which, in former days, very frequently the Prefect would exercise his men, but now only very seldom does he do so. "Soldiers" armed with the muzzle-loading gun of native or Chinese manufacture, also practise occasionally at a mark.

In every province there are "hunters," men who wear a particular kind of hat (a rough felt one with a conical crown), and a dark-blue coat, which are renewed annually by the King, and who also receive a small allowance of money, powder, and bullets from him; they are supposed to repay him by the skins and bodies of the game they slay. When the ravages of a man-eating tiger become too great, the King sometimes orders the hunters of several districts to join in an expedition against the monster. However unwilling to face it, they are obliged to go, and generally two or three of them get killed before the brute is despatched. They are liable to be called out for war, and in battle are selected to bear the brunt of the fighting; but preference is shown for those of the two Northern provinces, as being more inured to hardships and fatigue, and of better physique than those from the more Southern provinces, where the conditions of life are less rigorous.

The whole power of the State is vested really in the Prime Minister, who is of the Ming family, and a near relative of the

Queen, whose influence over the King is very great. Korea was only opened to foreigners in 1882, and the King has a "Foreign Adviser," General Le Gendre, an American, who prompts the King on matters of foreign policy. Strenuous efforts have been made to raise a Korean loan in America, but so far General Le Gendre and his royal pupil have not been able to offer sufficient security to get it taken up. The King likewise has a "Military Adviser," an office filled by General Dye, also an American, and, under the auspices of these advisers, foreigners of various nationalities have been brought to Korea to instruct the army. The present instructor at Soŭl, Colonel Nienstead, gave me much interesting information on Korean military matters; but, as I have before hinted, his enthusiasm for his duties led him to paint things in too glowing colours, and throw too favourable a light on the military administration (or maladministration) of the country.

The strength of the garrison of Soŭl is about 5000 men, divided into three divisions, each under a General, and there are five large barracks, in addition to smaller ones, for their accommodation. The conditions of service are purely voluntary, and although each man is supposed to do duty throughout the year, with the exception of the annual holiday before the drill season, which begins after the summer rains are over, about September, the duty actually performed is very little.

Three days on guard, three days in the country with his friends, then three days' drill, three days in the country, and so on, is not a very severe tax on him, especially as there is no punishment for failing to return to military duty. Each man receives a monthly allowance of pay and rice, but each General draws the pay for all under his command, and gives Treasury orders, generally six months in arrears, to his subordinates. As no questions are asked as to the numbers actually present and doing duty, I understand the General is expected to draw the full pay for his division and keep any balance arising from absentees for himself! Recruits learn simple movements very easily, and as they have a good ear for music, find no difficulty in learning bugle-calls. It is impossible, however, to teach them to march straight on a point. They are splendid pedestrians, as the following instances will show. At the funeral ceremony of the Japanese Envoy, a year or two ago, when the body was taken by land from Soŭl to Chémulpho, for shipment to Japan, the troops marched 25 miles in six hours. Again, on the occasion of the obsequies of the Queen Dowager in 1890, 600 men were brought from Phyŏng-yang by sea to Chémulpho, thence they marched to Soŭl, 24 miles, in six hours, and, without halting, proceeded in the cortège to the tomb, a further distance of 20 miles.

The officers must be of good birth, and pass through the Cadet College, as there is no promotion from the ranks; the only exceptions to this rule having been made in the case of two non-commissioned officers, who were made officers in 1888 as a reward of special merit; one died shortly afterwards of cholera, and the other becoming a Lieutenant, was appointed a magistrate. This employment being more profitable and congenial than soldiering, he declines to return to military duty. Of course, if any pressure were put on him by Korean authorities, he would show his wisdom by returning to his duty, rather than undergo the ignominious and painful ordeal of being conducted through the streets of the capital, while stalwart executioners beat him on the shins with cudgels, this being the punishment of delinquent officials. The duty of officers is nominally forty-eight hours in barracks or on guard, then forty-eight hours' leave, but practically they perform no duties at all, except to suit their own convenience.

The general opinion of the value of a Korean as a soldier is that he would be no good in the open, but would fight bravely behind cover, as was shown in the attempted American and French invasions in recent years. They are, in general, a well set-up race, of good physique, especially in the North, but are addicted to strong drink and debauchery, whenever they can afford such luxuries. The curse of the country is its form of government, which is modelled on the Chinese system, and is equally, if not more, antiquated, unwieldy, and corrupt. The people, to a foreigner, seem good-humoured, and display

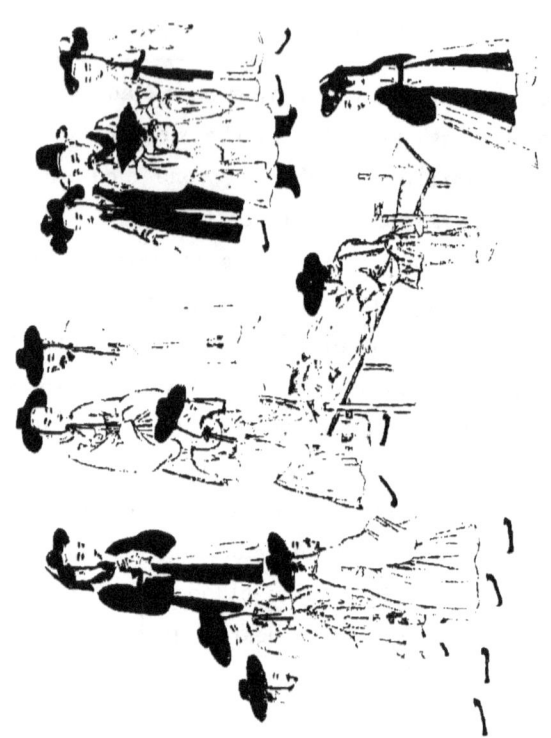

very little of that insane hatred of "barbarians" which is so conspicuous in China; but they are as conservative in their notions as the Chinese, and, seeing the small extent of their civilisation and industries, one wonders that they originally taught the Japanese the art of making pottery. Sanitary arrangements are entirely wanting, but the natives do not seem to suffer from the deficiency, and the country is by no means unhealthy.

The trade of Korea is steadily increasing, as may be seen from these figures. In 1888 foreign imports were valued at $3,046,443, and in 1890 at $4,727,839; exports to foreign countries for those years were valued at $867,058 and $3,550,478 respectively; while the net revenue from Customs dues in 1888 was $267,215, in 1890 it was $514,600, but 1890 was a year rejoicing in a favourable harvest of cereals, while the rice crop in Japan was bad. Of the imports in 1890, it may interest Britons to know that 57 per cent. were of British origin, 19 per cent. Japanese, 12 per cent. Chinese, and the rest German, American, Russian, French, and Austrian. A good deal of trade is done in the export of fish, salted, dried, or for manure, which amounted in 1890 to over $434,000 worth. The seas round Korea swarm with fish, and near Won-san I was told the water was at times literally stiff with the little fish used as manure by the Japanese, and which appears every two years; but the natives are so very lazy about sea-fishing, that they will go out for a few hours, make a good haul, and not go out again until the proceeds are spent, when very likely the shoals of fish have passed on. On the other hand, Japanese fishing-boats, which by a treaty have to pay for a license to fish within the three-mile limit, make good profits, the average earnings per boat during twelve months being £100. The Ming-Tai, a kind of haddock, which is caught on the east coast, north of Pukchöng, and dried without being salted, is a very favourite food; Won-san exporting to Korean ports no less than $359,000 worth. Whale-fishing is carried on outside Fu-san by Japanese whalers, who employ a large net to entangle the flippers and tail of the fish, to prevent it diving or damaging their boats. The Chinese from Shantung also catch large quantities of herrings off the west coast. Beans are becoming largely grown in Korea, for the demand for them in Japan is increasing, as they are used in the manufacture of Bean-curd, Miso, and Soy, while the Japanese are growing instead mulberries for sericulture. Wheat, barley, and rice, the latter of two kinds, one of which grows in dry soil, are also increasing, the export of these in 1890 being—barley, 5,260,533 lbs., value $50,341; beans, 87,950,800 lbs., value $1,004,762; wheat, 5,869,466 lbs., value $60,381; rice, 116,622,000 lbs., value $2,057,868. The manufacture of paper from the fibre of *Broussonetia papyrifera* is another growing industry, and from its durability and strength is much valued in China; the supply is not as yet equal to the demand, though mills are in course of erection near Soŭl; the export trade in this commodity in 1890 amounted to 149,891 lbs., value $26,244. Mills for cleaning and hulling rice have been erected at Chémulpho and Fu-san.

As a sign of the increase in foreign relations, the nationality of the foreign residents in the three treaty ports is shown in the table below.

	Chémulpho.	Fu-san.	Won-san.	Total.
American	4	...	...	4
Austrian	3	...	...	3
British	7	4	2	13
Chinese	425 (in 1888—242)	47 (in 1888—31)	45 (in 1888—26)	517
Danish	...	...	1	1
French	2	...	...	2
German	19	2	2	23
Italian	1	1	...	2
Japanese	1616 (in 1888—1359)	4130 (in 1888—2711)	689 (in 1888—453)	6435
Spanish	1	...	...	1
Total	2078	4184	739	7001

CHAPTER III.

SOŬL TO WON-SAN.

ON Saturday, September 5th, twenty-two days since we left Hong-Kong, we were able to start on our land-journey, a really

READY TO START.

clear sky giving promise of better weather. To our surprise, for we had been told that ponies never turned up at the time agreed on, our animals arrived early, and we had all our baggage loaded by 8 A.M., after much wrangling about the division of the loads, the total weight of everything coming to about 1100 lbs. The pack-saddle consists of two arches joined at the sides by cross-pieces of wood; this frame is placed on a pad stuffed with straw, and then the boxes are put on in this fashion:—A large loop is made in a rope and laid across the saddle, a box is lifted to each side, the loop passed over one box, then the ends of the rope through the loop, under the box on the other side, and up to the end of the loop, pulled tight and fastened in a knot. On the top of the saddle other smaller articles are placed, and then a hide surcingle is put round the whole and securely tied. There is a good deal of art involved in getting the load to balance equally and in tying it to the saddle. A breastplate and a crupper serve to keep the load from slipping forward and back to a great extent. However, galls where the weight comes on the shoulder and loins and at the root of the tail are usual. We found that our pony-bridles were much too large for the small ponies we were to ride, while the delay was increased by the breaking of Goold-Adams' girths. My pony was certainly not more than eleven hands high, and was destitute of withers and shoulders, but did not stumble frightfully, like Goold-Adams' beast, which, on the other hand, could walk faster. Having got repairs executed to the girths and reefs taken in our bridles, we mounted, and, after two photographs of our cavalcade had been taken by Mr.

Hillier, we were fairly off by 9.35 A.M. Mr. Hillier's temporary abode was built on a terrace cut in the hillside, whence a flight of about twenty steps led to the outer yard and entrance gate. Notwithstanding the clever way the loaded ponies walked down these steps, we could not at starting harden our hearts enough to ride down them, so we walked down and mounted at the entrance-gate, waving farewell to our kind and hospitable host and the Italian Consul. Slowly we threaded our way through the narrow muddy streets to the east gate of the city, jostled continually by the numerous ponies and bulls passing along, laden with dried fish, country produce, or brushwood for fuel for the "kang" or stove. These animals were in strings of from two to six, following at uncertain intervals one as a leader who seemed to know his way, while the drivers stopped every minute to light their pipes, to exchange a little gossip with an acquaintance, or to snatch a mouthful of food in one of the numerous booths for the sale of curious and not-to-be-inquired-into-too-closely-looking viands. The main streets, running to the four points of the compass, are fairly wide, but booths and shanties are allowed to encroach a great deal on the road space, and reduce the width materially. However, when the King goes out in the city, these structures have to be removed by their owners.

The east gate is a somewhat imposing structure, occupying about 40 yards of the city wall, while the passage in the

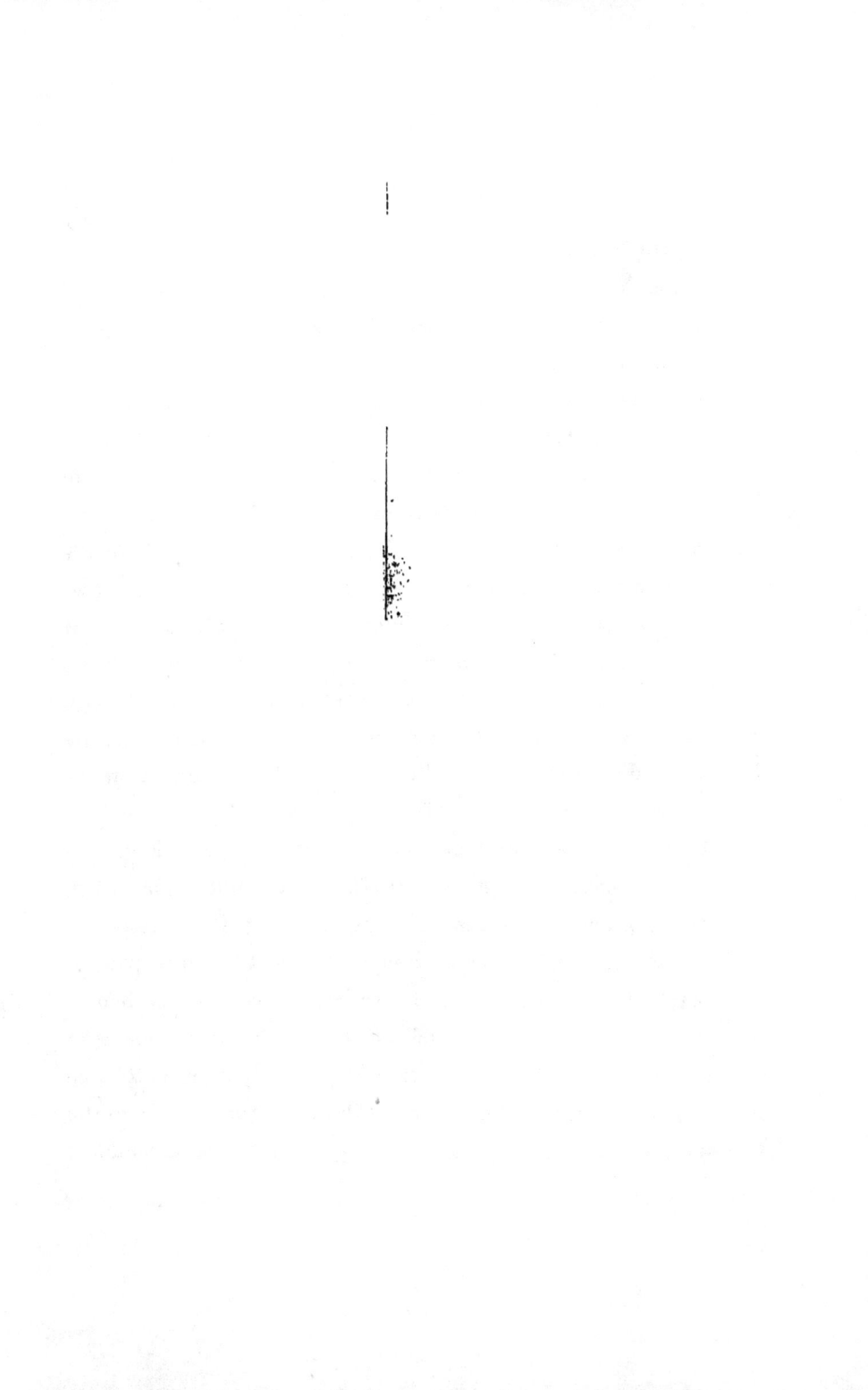

centre is about 30 feet wide and 20 feet high to the top of the arch; above the arch, which is on a level with the top of the wall, here about 15 feet thick, is a wooden gallery, with a curled roof of tiles, whence the surrounding country can be watched; the woodwork is painted in bright colours, with royal and official emblems, and on the whole, when compared with the squalid huts and cabins beneath it, the gate is not without dignity and stateliness. A mound of earth 15 feet high faced with stone starts from the right-hand side of the gateway, and coming round in an arc, forms a kind of outer traverse to the entrance. We passed through this gate at 10.15 A.M., leaving the capital of Korea with its 250,000 inhabitants behind us, and journeyed along the plain, through which a tributary of the Han flows, until 3.50 P.M., when we stopped for the night at Wi-erh-mi, a little village of twelve houses and an inn. The fertility of this valley surprised us, for we had been told that Koreans cultivated as little ground as possible; but here were rice-fields in endless succession, giving promise of a good harvest, though the quality of the rice is not equal to the Japanese; excellent hemp in patches beside the numerous small hamlets of two to six houses which we passed, each patch enough for the requirements of the owners, with a small margin for trading purposes; tobacco 7 or 8 feet high, with long coarse leaves bearing witness to the want of care in its cultivation, while castor-oil plants bordered the little garden plots of chillies, cabbages, and turnips, which we found outside each house or collection of houses. Besides flax, maize, and cotton, there were fields of the small millet (*Setaria italica*), substitute for porridge, and of the tall millet, Susu or Kaoliang (*Holcus Sorghum*), with stems 8 to 12 feet high and as thick as a man's thumb, turning to golden yellow or bright mahogany colour; from the latter kind the Koreans make the coarse cloth of which their rough garments are composed, when they do not use Manchester shirtings; also fields of beans, food for cattle and men, and the foundation of Japanese soy and our Worcestershire sauce. Many of the houses had their roofs covered with gourds, while here and there were patches of melons. In the villages, a little way off the road, we could see fruit-trees, pear, persimmon, and peach, but in those on the road very seldom did we come across any. All the fruit except the Ham-heung pears was hard, dry, and tasteless. The valley of this tributary stream, being some 2 miles wide and shut in by bare foot-hills 50 to 300 feet high, overlooked by equally bare mountains 300 to 1000 feet in height, and besides having a very slight fall towards the sea, is very liable to floods, which, however, subside as quickly as they rise. At the base of the foot-hills the road winds about, rapidly narrowing about 15 miles from Soŭl to a mere bridle-path, and we found our chief obstacles in the constant climbing over the water-channels which are constructed to

carry off the water from the hills, and whence the irrigation of the rice-fields is conducted. Some of these were 10 to 30 yards broad, with a few inches of water flowing over a sandy bed; others were simple dykes.

Up to 2 P.M. we pursued a north-easterly course along the Soŭl-Won-san high-road, which is a tolerably good track in fine weather, but was now very muddy and boggy in places, its course marked by the telegraph line. At that hour we stopped at a little hamlet to obtain some fresh shoes for the ponies, and just after leaving again, our "mapus" or drivers branched off the high-road towards the N.N.E., taking one which is known as the "short road." As this looked infinitely better than the main track, we did not notice the divergence, although along the latter were still coming strings of bulls and ponies. Altogether during our day's march I counted over 300 ponies and 160 bulls bound for the capital. The reason for this deviation we ascertained at Won-san afterwards, and this was that the "mapus" thought they would be paid more by us, as the time occupied this way would be greater than by the proper road. However, they were deceived in their expectations.

On arriving at Wi-erh-mi, which was reckoned as 60 li or about 18 miles from Soŭl, we pitched our tent in a graveyard, on a mound 20 feet above the road, and close to the little inn. The Koreans, like the Chinese, generally bury their dead on the spur of a hill, raising a circular mound of earth over the grave, some 4 feet high and 6 feet in diameter; this and the surrounding ground is planted with grass and carefully kept clear of brushwood; occasionally carved stone images are placed on each side of the grave, and often they are at the extremities of a grass terrace in front of it. We observed that these graves protected the trees in their immediate vicinity from the destruction which the demand for firewood in populous districts caused; for we very frequently found a ring or copse of large pines or oaks surrounding a grave, when there was not a single tree more than 3 feet in height anywhere within sight, except at similar sacred spots on the hill-tops. We carefully inquired if we should hurt the feelings of the natives by encamping here, but learnt it was a matter of absolute indifference to them; wherefore we unloaded our ponies on the newly-mown grass, and, after showing the servants how to pitch the tent and arrange our beds and baggage in it, we left the cook to get dinner for us at 7 P.M. Goold-Adams taking a rod and I a gun, we went down to the river, about 300 yards off, across the rice-fields. It was a lovely evening, with a soft warm breeze from the south-west. The river, a tributary of the Han, was about 40 yards wide, not more than 2 feet deep, flowing about $1\frac{1}{2}$ miles an hour over a sandy bed. We could see that it was easily fordable in several places, but an embankment about 4 feet high ran along our side of its bed, about 40 yards from the water's edge, and up a small stream flowing into it, to keep it when iu flood from sweeping away the rice-fields, which lay between it and the foot of the hills. From the small tributary stream Goold-Adams took two tiny trout, which he gave to a little boy, whom we had bribed to carry our produce of the chase. Alas! I only saw a water-hen and two wood-pigeons, which were too wily to come within shot, and we returned hungry and disappointed to our camp. The mosquitoes were troublesome in the early part of the night, but later a mist rose from the damp fields and lessened their attacks. At 9 P.M., when we went to bed, the thermometer showed 68° out of doors.

Notwithstanding that our three servants slept outside the tent, under a shelter improvised from the tent-ropes and a couple of waterproof sheets, they did not hurry themselves next morning very much about preparations for starting; what with the slowness of the cook about our breakfast, the time they consumed over their own subsequent "chow," and the quarrels of the "mapus" over the different loads, it was 8.45 A.M. before we were started. Later on we rectified this waste of time to a great extent, but it was impossible to obviate it entirely, as a Korean is absolutely ignorant of, or indifferent to, the value of time. We began to ascend and descend the low spurs running down to the river, which till 10.30 A.M. continued to flow on our right in a southerly direction. Much to our astonishment, after passing through a small wood and stream, and over a stony spur certainly not 100 feet above the main stream, but stretching down to it, we arrived at the bank of a river exactly like the one of last night, but it was flowing to the north. Our maps did not help us, and the only solution of the mystery we could arrive at, without searching for their sources, was that the stony spur stretched across the valley and formed the water-parting between the two streams, each rising from the hills, the first on our left and the new one on our right. We crossed the stream, a tributary of the Im-jin, and again at 1 o'clock by a ford 2½ feet deep, where the water was flowing at the rate of 3 miles an hour, over a bed of slippery boulders. We halted for luncheon at a small village on the right bank, and going immediately a little way down-stream, enjoyed a splendid bathe, though the water was not deep enough to swim in without knocking oneself against the stones, which again were too slippery to stand on. As we had gradually forged ahead of our baggage-train, being unable to endure the slow pace at which they went, we had to dry ourselves by the aid of the sun's rays and our pocket-handkerchiefs. Our luncheon of corned beef, hard-boiled eggs, and whisky was brought to us in a small clump of trees close by, and at 3 o'clock we were off again. We were so disgusted at the slowness of the "mapus," who strolled along at the rate of 8 li an hour, that we adopted the plan of walking for an hour and then riding for an hour, accompanied by one "mapu," who drove our ponies after us, and we found we could maintain easily an average of 10 li an hour. On almost every road we travelled, we met, 10 li apart, wooden posts, stuck up by the roadside, surmounted by a grotesquely carved human face, with an inscription giving the distance from the capital and the nearest town. These li-posts, called Chang-sung, are marvels of hideousness, and are said to be dedicated to a very strong man, and a noted robber in olden times, whose spirit is supposed to haunt the road.

Still through cultivation, and getting nearer the main chain of mountains which traverses Korea from north to south, we pursued a rough path until 6 o'clock, when shortly after crossing a deep, swift stream, we had to climb up a path cut in the face of a precipice overhanging the river Im-jin—a most dangerous corner, where the ponies had sôme difficulty in getting up the slippery rock; safely passed, we turned away from the river, down to a few houses in a small valley beside a rivulet. In one of these we saw a naked boy four or five years old taking the natural nourishment of infancy from his mother, as she sat engaged in some household occupation at the open door. Again surmounting a rocky and wooded spur, we descended to a ferry over the Im-jin. The mountains had now closed in on us, and these cliffs were all on the left bank of the river, which here made a great bend. After some parley between our "mapu" and the ferryman, we got on board the boat, which, rectangular in plan, was composed of a flat bottom of planks, with upright sides about two feet high, the ends being sloped off to admit of its being got near the banks, and to facilitate the embarkation and disembarkation of cattle and ponies, whose cleverness in getting in and out, though heavily laden, is remarkable. One man "uloed," that is, he propelled the boat by means of a long sweep working in a hollow in the end of the boat, another poled us along the bank up a back-water formed by the swift current impinging on a projecting rocky bluff. As we got into the current, it caught the front end of the boat (bow and stern being exactly alike), and we crossed the river, here 100 yards wide, diagonally and downwards, until we got into another back-water on the opposite side, which brought us safely to land opposite our starting-point. Like all the ferry-boats, this one leaked at a rate most alarming to us, but after a time this leaking, with many other things, we came to regard as part of the day's work. On landing we gave the ferryman a silver Japanese 20-sen piece, worth about eightpence, at which he grumbled, not knowing what it was, and passing through the little hamlet near the ferry, we waited on the top of the hill for the rest of our party. In half-an-hour I saw them crossing the river, and walking down to the ferry, found everything safe, but the ferryman was still objecting to the silver coin; so I gave him instead 100 cash or about sixpence, at which he was pleased. Going a mile farther, we came to the little village of Chan-go-ra-ni, and again found an excellent camping-ground in a graveyard with two graves on a hillock overlooking the village and the river. The inhabitants with one accord turned out to inspect us and our tent, which was an object none of them had ever seen before; so intense was their curiosity, that, even when we closed the doors to change our clothes, we could not look up without finding an eye glued to a hole in the lacing, and every few minutes a stampede told us the crowd of sightseers was being chased away by our servants. Our ponies and "mapus" put up at the inn in the village.

We found that as we got farther from Soŭl and nearer the main chain of mountains, the hills began to lose the desolate and shaven appearance we had hitherto noticed, and their sides and summits to be clothed with pine-trees of no great height, while the lower slopes had a small growth of stunted oaks and pines two or three feet high; the rivers no longer meandered through an alluvial plain, covered with rice-fields, but began to flow between an old river-bed on one side, and a more or less precipitous hillside on the other. The fertility of these river-beds was surprising, and we were astonished not to find more animal and bird life amongst the fields and trees, for only a few snipe and a wood-pigeon or two rewarded our anxious searching. We suffered a great loss to-day; owing to the carelessness of one of the "mapus," his pony, in fighting with another, kicked a case of whisky, and alas! broke a bottle.

Soon after leaving Chan-go-ra-ni next morning, we crossed a small stream, and had a stiff climb of 200 feet up a very rocky path on to a small plateau of lava, which gradually descended towards the river, and four hours later we stopped at 11.30 A.M. for the midday halt at a small village on the bank. We painfully toiled over the boulders to the edge of the water, fortunately finding a stranded tree on which to sit, and here we bathed and had our luncheon. The water being delightfully cold, freshened us up immensely, for our ablutions, morning and night, from pressure of time and space, and the numerous male and female eyes vigilantly on the watch, were somewhat limited, the apparatus available being, besides soap, &c., a small tin basin and a minute supply of hot water for each. After luncheon we endeavoured to find a place of rest, but in vain. The people do not, except on rare occasions, use seats, but squat on their heels, while their habits in sanitary matters, and the cultivation of every available scrap of ground, render it almost impossible to find a patch of grass on which to sit. We were tormented here by flies in shape and size like the ordinary

川喜田半泥子

house-fly, but grey in colour, which took a special liking to Goold-Adams, biting him through his breeches and stockings in a most ferocious manner, the wounds remaining sore for days after; these flies were only near the river-side villages, and in two days we ceased to meet with them.

By 2 P.M. we were again on the march along the fertile valley of the river Im-jin, and during the afternoon we crossed the stream no less than seven times, but towards sunset we left it on our left, and crossing a plain about two miles wide covered with blocks of lava, we ascended a pass in the hills which was 785 feet above the sea. At the summit we saw, for the first time, a tree dedicated to the spirit of the hills, one of a group of pine-trees, with numerous scraps of rag fastened to its branches and a heap of stones at its foot, which formed the votive offerings of travellers. We descended to the village of Hang-na-dou-ché-ra-noup, finding a camping-place on the side of a hill at its farther boundary, just above the inn, the graveyard this time failing to afford us level ground. It was quite dark before our tent was ready for us, as the baggage-ponies did not come up until 6.30 P.M. Ché-ra-noup being a place containing thirty houses, we were soon surrounded by a crowd of gaping villagers, perfectly good-humoured, but determined to see everything they could. The head man of the village came in the evening to know if we wanted to see him; but as we were just getting into bed, we said we would not trouble him, and only wanted the crowd to go away, which he kindly persuaded it to do about 8.30 P.M.

During the morning I saw a very handsome snake, about two feet long, crossing the road almost under my pony's feet; the head was black, while for half its length the back was bright orange, gradually merging into bright green, and a diamond-shaped black-marking ran down it: in the afternoon I caught sight of a brown adder about 1½ feet long, and promptly despatched the poisonous reptile with my stick.

Making an early start at 7 A.M. on the morning of the 8th, we embarked on a plain of lava some fourteen miles wide, gradually sloping upwards in a N.N.E. direction. The track was infamous, blocks of lava sticking up in all directions, while at intervals of about half-an-hour we came to boggy places, through which our ponies floundered with difficulty. The previous evening it had commenced to rain, and continued to do so at intervals during the night, and during the day we encountered several heavy showers, which made the road worse. The plain was covered with a thick growth of coarse grass, and dotted with dwarf pines and oaks, stunted in their growth by continual cutting down for firewood and the shallowness of the soil; the oak leaves were in some cases 12 inches long and 5 inches broad, and wild rosemary and strawberry plants covered the ground. I saw one or two ripe berries of the latter, but did not dismount to gather them, and perhaps it was as well I did not, for at Won-san we were told they were called "snake-strawberries," and were poisonous to mankind. We stopped for luncheon at Phyöng-yang-hwa, a small and dirty village, and stayed there till 1 P.M., utilising part of the time by crossing the stream, which was flowing to the south on our right beneath the edge of the plain, by a rough causeway of boulders, to look for pheasants, but failed to see any. On resuming our journey, Goold-Adams and I walked on along the main track for an hour, till our "mapu" caught us up with our steeds, and told us we were going the wrong road, having passed the right one, which was a little bridle-path to the left, just after leaving the village. He knew what he was about, for he led us across country in a N.N.W. direction to a river flowing east, evidently the Hoi-yang river, a tributary of the Han; the river was deep, rapid, and perfectly clear, and we kept along its right bank for some time. In its winding course, the river was rapidly eating away the cultivated land on one bank, but in compensation adding stones and sand to the opposite one. We had to cross this stream twice, and had some difficulty in finding a ford shallow enough for us to do so in safety. Turning away from

E

the river to the left, we gradually climbed up 1000 feet to a range of hills composed of disintegrating granite slightly mixed with lava. On arriving at the summit, about 1500 feet above the sea, we saw beneath us a lovely valley, with the large village of Phyöng-yang nestling under the shelter of what had once been the precipitous bank of the river. This comes round in an arc, completely shielding the place from the cold north and north-west winds, which at times make the winter cold almost unbearable. Between the village and the river was a stretch of alluvial soil, about a quarter of a mile wide and a mile long, on which we saw growing crops of rice, millet, beans, and tobacco. An hour later we got to Tang-na-ri, a village of thirty-five houses, which, with a few fields, was surrounded by a belt of pine-trees, a small stream flowing through its midst. The only place we could find for our tent was the northern edge of the trees, by the roadside, and the cold north wind blowing through our wet clothes made us feel decidedly chilly, though at 9 P.M. the thermometer showed 61°. Fortunately the cold served to drive away the shivering sightseers earlier than usual. During the day we put up a couple of pheasants, but of course our guns were with the other baggage, pursuing the right road; we also saw in the morning some long strings of white cranes. Our Chinese cook distinguished himself by falling off his pony three times to-day, owing to its stumbling. Mr. Carles, in his account of his journey in 1884, mentions the same peculiarity on the part of our cook, who accompanied him, and gives his age then as about fifty-five! To us he did not look as if he was sixty-two, but the age of a Chinaman is very difficult to guess without a long acquaintance with the people. Our dinner, however, in spite of his age and bruises, was not the less well cooked. There appeared to be some hesitation amongst the servants about sleeping outside the tent, no doubt influenced by the cold wind and our proximity to the mountains, which were reported to be infested with tigers.

The following morning, hearing from the villagers that there were many pheasants around the village, we took our guns, and started at 7.30 to look for them. Yeung had procured a man who professed to know where the birds were likely to be found, but our labour was in vain, for not a bird or beast did we see. After beating many fields of beans and millet, and crossing many rivulets hidden in swamp and long grass which soaked us to the waist, we gave up the pursuit in disgust after an hour's fruitless toil, and returned to the highroad, to find that our "mapu" had taken our ponies on with the others, instead of waiting for us, as we had told him to do. We had therefore a weary tramp of one and a half hours along a lava-strewn path, varied by bogs, through which we had to wade the best way we could. Our tempers when we found our "mapu" quietly sitting smoking at a wayside inn were none of the best, and Yeung, whose cotton trousers and socks were wet and muddy, required little urging to give him a broadside of Korean abuse. We stopped for two hours at 11.30 A.M. for midday feeding, and the sun coming out, kindly dried our wet clothes. Just before 4 P.M. we reached the edge of this great plain of lava, which terminated in the gorge of a river flowing north, into which we were about to descend; on our left was a huge cliff going sheer down to the river some 500 feet below. Whence this vast lava plain, many feet deep and miles wide, could have come from, we were unable to conjecture, for we could see nothing approaching a crater amongst the mountains in sight; but as this plain rises towards the chain of mountains here, and that on the northern side falls away from it, their origin must have been hereabouts. These lava plains are not wholly destitute of cultivation; here and there, near the rivers which bordered them, we saw fields of millet and beans, and on the farther banks were many small hamlets and some considerable villages; but our attendants professed entire ignorance of the names of these, and of the rivers and mountains in sight; neither had they any idea where the gold-washings, which we knew were not far off, could be found. This ignorance was annoying, as the road had not previously, as far as I could learn, been travelled by a European. The difficulty in ascertaining names of localities is intensified by the playful habit the inhabitants of each district bordering on a river or a chain of mountains have of giving their own names to them; hence a river may have five or six names in a course of a hundred miles, and after a little we gave up asking the names, and by keeping a watch on the formation of the surrounding country, we managed to identify the main streams which we passed.

Through a narrow cut in the edge of the plain, we wound our way down a rough path, which we found most toilsome to travel on foot, and after descending 400 feet we came upon a gateway of wood some 6 feet wide and 8 feet high, with a gallery above as a look-out, placed in a stone wall about 6 feet thick and 10 feet high, running from the cliff above the river up a spur to the top of the ridge on our right. This fortification, dilapidated of course, marked the boundary-line between the provinces of Kang-wŏn and Ham-gyŏng, which latter we now entered. Passing through this gateway, we kept along the gorge of the river, about 200 feet above it, but it rapidly narrowed, forcing us to descend to the right bank, past a couple of houses, which, from the number of beehives posted about the rocks, appeared to constitute a bee-farm. The hives consist of a log of wood two feet long, partially hollowed out, and placed on end in a crevice in the rocks with a piece of board on top, kept in place by a large stone, a small hole being left for the bees to go in and out. There must have been a hundred of these about, but on offering to buy some honey, we were told we could get none till next moon.

The river, which, as we heard, had the day before been quite impassable owing to the rain, was still flowing swiftly about 2½ feet deep over a bed of boulders; the water too was icy cold, and my little rat of a pony was nearly swept away, as he was submerged as far as half-way up the saddle-flaps. Getting safely over, we waited to see the whole train across, and every instant expected to see a pony and some of our precious stores swept away; but the "mapus," tucking up their trousers as high as they could, waded beside the clever little beasts, encouraging them by much voice and a little whip, and everything came over safe and dry. We now learnt that one of the baggage-ponies was stone blind, and we marvelled how he managed to get across the river and through the next day's march as he did without falling. The cook, being a bad pedestrian, had been left some way behind in the descent, and on arriving at the brink of the ford, found his pony had already crossed; there was no help for it, so he had to strip to the waist, and pick his way across barefooted. The disgusted expression of his face sent us into such fits of laughter, that, to avoid hurting his feelings, we moved on. Twice more had we to ford this river in the twilight, and just as it became dark we stopped at the village of Tan-ga-ni, which was perched on the left bank, on a terrace formed in

ancient days by the river deposits. Every inch of soil being cultivated, we had to pitch our tent on the village threshing-floor in front of one of the houses; the ground was covered with fleas, and these, with the talking in the house a few feet away, kept us awake for some time. Across the river, on the same level, 25 feet above the stream, at intervals, were similar cultivated terraces; towering some thousand feet above us were the mountains clothed with sombre pines, and here and there near the water a small oak-tree.

"Just the place for a tiger," said we, and were not surprised at being told the inhabitants often saw one in winter, or at our servants preferring to sleep in a house. It was just as well they did so, as it poured during the night. We, however, enjoyed a sound sleep, disturbed only by a stray pony falling over our tent-ropes, which projected into the roadway, and nearly bringing our canvas house about our ears. I noticed here that the village curs were shut up at night, significant of visits from tigers and leopards. We afterwards learnt that the mountains between us and the sea swarmed with these beasts, and that several deaths had occurred from carelessness in moving about after dark. Some travellers, who had been visiting the Buddhist monasteries in these mountains to the south-east, just about this time, told us they had been shown the place where a monk had been seized and devoured by a tiger, only a few days previous to their visit, and traces of the accident were still plainly visible.

The answer, next morning, to our daily inquiry as to halting-places, was that there was only one inn in a space of 130 li, that the road was very bad, and therefore we would do the day's journey without halting. The result was that we did not get off until nearly nine o'clock, and we soon found that "very bad" was far too good a description of what was called a road! We were absolutely unable to ride for more than a quarter of a mile during a march of four and a half hours! I may state here that roads, as understood by Western minds, do not exist in Korea; the communications by land consist of bridle and footpaths, worn by traffic to such degree of passability as they possess. Only stern necessity ever causes any repairs to be executed on a road; though, in a few instances, I noticed the track was being widened, and holes in the soft soil filled in, to permit the sleds to pass along in winter, without undue strain from contact with the uneven frozen surface. Generally the track follows a watercourse; though, on the coast, where the rivers are mostly shallow and with wide beds, it has to cross the streams.

The track wound along the left bank of the river, shut in between the mountains, which increased in height as we progressed; up rocky spurs, fifty to a hundred feet above the river, and down again to its bed, we had one continual clamber over rocks and boulders; now a few feet above the water, now along a shelf in the cliff twenty to fifty feet above it; overhanging rocks, in places where the river was slowly eating away the cliffs, or where the loosening effect of severe frost, heavy rains, and burning sun had caused recent landslips, seemed on the point of falling on us, and on this account we were rather pleased to leave, at length, the river gorge. In compensation for our toil, the scenery was magnificent in its savage beauty; granite mountains on either bank towered 1500 feet above us, some bare of trees to their summits, others clothed with pine-trees, all covered with a carpet of tall coarse grass and weeds, down to where they abruptly ended in precipices, with the rushing, noisy river bathing their feet. Down in the narrow lateral glens, scored by the mountain torrents, small oaks and maples found a precarious footing in the rocky sides. At one place a dyke of granite almost bridged the stream, leaving only one narrow gap 10 yards across, through which the river, here 50 yards wide and 8 to 10 feet deep, boiled, a mass of foam 20 feet below, the roar of its passage echoed and re-echoed rendering conversation almost impossible. A summer flood here would indeed be a grand sight!

About noon we turned up a glen along a zigzag path newly cut in the mountain-side, the old path, now become the bed of a mountain torrent, having to be abandoned.

We thought it high time we got a little value out of our ponies, so made them carry us half-way up the ascent of 800 feet, but we had to walk the remainder. At the top we rested awhile to give men and ponies time to get breath, and thence, by a fairly good track, reached the little village of An-pyön, the prefectural town of that name being some distance to the north-east. Here for the first time we came upon a real bridge. We had indeed crossed two torrents by means of four or five planks laid side by side, but this village possessed a single-arch bridge, built of rough stone with no mortar. Whilst waiting for our baggage-ponies to come up, we were invited by the villagers to rest in their houses, offering us at the same time unripe pears and peaches, with which the trees were loaded, and seemed much puzzled at our refusals; their perplexity was relieved when they saw our tent pitched in the centre of the village, on the only level spot we could find. After carefully sweeping the ground, we sprinkled it with a strong solution of permanganate of potash, and then powdered it with Keating's insect powder, for the fleas and flies were in myriads. After luncheon we went a little way down the stream to a sandy spot near a water-mill, and enjoyed a delicious bathe, not without being spied out by the village children, who watched us from the bank. This mill (Mul-pang-a) was the first of the kind we saw, as the harvest had hardly yet commenced. A tree-trunk is hollowed out to a trough at one end, and is so balanced on a pair of trunnions set in a frame, that when the trough is filled by water led to it from the neighbouring stream, the trough-end sinks, the water is discharged, and the log resumes its place; the other end, being fitted with a wooden peg, acts as a pestle on the grain, placed in a mortar sunk in the ground. This takes place six to nine times a minute. In some places farther north, we saw ten or twenty of these

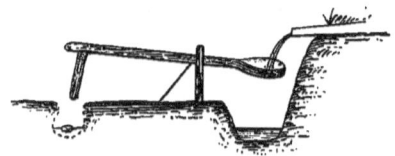

ROUGH SKETCH OF WATER-MILL.

mills at work, and the creaking of their trunnions was most doleful. Smaller mills are worked by the foot on precisely the same principle, and I saw similar mills afterwards at work in Japan. I noticed to-day quantities of wild raspberries, and everywhere on the high ground grew the wild rosemary, while the rocks were covered with the pretty creeper (*Ampelopsis Veitchii*).

We were now close to the main road again, and were much surprised when the "mapus" said we could not get to Won-san next day, there being only one halting place in the next

110 li. As we had only done 50 li to-day, we began to suspect the delay was intentional.

Starting on Friday morning at 8.30 A.M., we crossed another lava plain, gradually descending to a feeder of yesterday's river, and during the morning we got into the high-road from Soül, which we had left on the 5th. There was more traffic now, for we were constantly meeting bulls and ponies coming from Won-san laden with bundles of dried fish, while for three days previously we had encountered only two ponies. After a march of 4¾ hours we descended a slight declivity to Nam-san, which consisted of one long street close to the right bank of the river. On the other side of the village was an oval plain of alluvial soil very gradually sloping to the river, and every inch of this was under cultivation; so much so that we were unable to find a spot on which to pitch the tent, and very reluctantly we had to go to a Korean house. The room we were given was about 7 feet wide, 20 feet long, and 6½ feet high; at one end a small door led into the stable, which was also the kitchen; on the right two doors of lattice-work covered with paper opened into the street, and on the left another door led into a smaller room, where our servants were to sleep; at the opposite end of the room another door opened into the street in an angle with the garden-wall, beneath which an open drain took its way to the main thoroughfare.

The walls of the house were of wattle and daub, between rough-hewn uprights, while the mud floor was covered with straw-mats; the roof was supported by heavy timbers, out of all proportion in weight to the uprights, and vastly in excess of the strain imposed by the light thatch roof. Behind the house was a little garden, where grew a patch of chillies, some cabbages, turnips, and gourds.

We staved off the curiosity of the villagers by shutting the doors and windows; but as the good lady of the house had lighted the "kang" and it was a hot afternoon, we were half stifled. Hastily swallowing our luncheon, we sallied forth, accompanied by Yeung and a man who said he could show us heaps of pheasants. Our guide carried us across the river, which was about two feet deep, one by one on his back, then we tramped over several hills and through fields without finding a trace of anything, forded another stream, and finally were told by the Koreans, of whom two more had joined us, that they knew of a place where a big tiger was seen every day by a boy as he went to his work; they even pointed out the place to us, a low sandy hill partially covered with pine-trees; but when we announced our intention of going to look for the animal, they began to prevaricate, saying they were not sure on which hill or when it was last seen, and finally refused to come with us. We had intended to walk to the An-pyön monastery, some 10 li farther on, a large place with a very fine avenue of old trees, which we could see at the foot of the mountains, across what is called the An-pyön plain; but it was now (five o'clock) too late, so we turned off to look for the tiger, accompanied only by the unfortunate Yeung. In passing over the hill indicated to us, we came upon the fresh track of a leopard going towards the plain, but soon lost it in the scrub, also one pheasant, which, though winged, we lost in the grass. There were numerous tracks of tiger-cats and deer, but we saw nothing of the beasts themselves.

Returning to our house, we found it still so unbearably hot that we had to open all the doors and windows, and change our wet clothes in full view of the passers-by. The thermometer being at $85°$, and no means of ventilation existing, we asked to have the "kang" put out, which with great difficulty we got done, as our servants wished to enjoy the warmth of it. The "kang" is a simple and inexpensive way of warming the house, universal in Korea. A small fire of brushwood is lighted in a small furnace at one end or side of the house; thence numerous flues under the mud floor conduct the smoke and hot air to an upright chimney or a hole in the wall at the opposite end or side, and very little fire suffices to thoroughly heat a large house. The Chinese "kang" is on the same principle, but the flue forms a raised bench along one side of the rooms. I was not surprised, later on, to find that coughs and colds were very common, for an indoor temperature between 70° and 80°, and an outdoor one of 0°, form very trying extremes. Moreover, the constant warmth serves to keep alive the numerous flies, fleas, bugs, and cockroaches, with which most of the houses swarm.

Saturday, September 12th, was occupied by our eighth march, in doing a distance which ordinarily by the right road takes five or six days! However, at Soŭl we had met two German officers who had just come overland from Won-san by the high-road, and they had been kept five days at one place by a swollen river; so at any rate we had more luck than they. We started at 7.45 A.M., and forded the river at once, as usual in the deepest and most difficult part of the ford, an almost invariable custom on the part of our "mapus." Having despatched the baggage on in front, and whilst waiting for our riding-ponies by the water's edge, I noticed a Korean woman crossing the river with a baby slung on her back at a different part of the ford, the water barely reaching her knees in the deepest part, while our ponies were floundering in water deeper by a foot. The method of carrying infants is simple: the child is seated in a strip of cloth, the ends of which pass round the mother's neck and cross over her breast, the child's legs embracing her waist.

Climbing up the steep river-bank, we came out on to the continuation of the lava plain we had crossed yesterday, which was about 500 feet above the sea, and gradually sloped downwards in a northerly direction. Two miles off, on our left, was the upper part of the river we had just crossed, and on the farther bank I remarked an odd formation in a cliff above it; the granite strata were horizontal, but apparently a column of some other rock had been forced vertically upwards, causing the face of the cliff to assume a somewhat strange appearance.

On this plain was pointed out to us the site of a great battle between the Koreans and the Japanese during the invasion by the latter in 1592. Huge grass mounds, still carefully tended, mark the resting-place of the fallen warriors on both sides, and Yeung told us 18,000 men were killed in this battle. A curious little book, by a Japanese, which I bought in Yokohama, in giving extracts from the history of Korea, states that the tribute paid to Japan for many years consisted of one gold box containing ginseng, three beautiful horses, forty white falcons, one gold casket ornamented with pearls and other precious stones, which contained rolls or letters in the Korean language, and forty tiger-skins, the hair of which was a finger long; while the tribute to China, which she no longer enforces, owing to the poverty of her vassal, was 100 ounces of gold, 1000 ounces of silver, 10,000 sacks of rice, 2000 pieces of silk, 300 ditto of linen, 10,000 ditto of drill or cotton, 400 ditto of flax-cloth, 100 ditto of fine flax-cloth, 1000 rolls of two leaves each of large paper, 1000 rolls of small paper, 2000 good knives, 1000 bullock's horns, 40 mats with de-

signs, 200 lbs. of dye-wood, 10 bushels of pepper, 100 tiger-skins, 100 deer-skins, 400 beaver-skins, and 200 blue mole-skins.

About 11 A.M. we came to the edge of this plain, and descended to another covered with rice-fields, stretching inland to the hills about three miles on our left and for five or six miles round the bay, which was about three miles off to our right front. Large villages lay under these hills, and the road wound its dusty length across the plain, its course marked by the telegraph poles, the reappearance of which we had hailed with joy about two hours earlier. A small sluggish stream furnished the means of irrigation, but we could see that with heavy rain it flooded a great deal, in spite of the embankments, five or six feet high. We saw and heard snipe in all directions, and numerous storks and cranes were wading about in the rice-swamps. Soon the hills came nearer the shore, and the road wound about under them, shortly emerging on to another plain of rice, at the end of which we were glad to see the native town of Won-san. But before reaching the place we had to be ferried over two rivers, as the bridges were only just being put up again after the summer rains. The rivers being subject to heavy floods, the superstructure, and often the piles, are removed and stored away from May to September. The general form of bridge consists of a series of pairs of piles driven into the river-bed, bratticed together by cross-pieces,

F

while the superstructure consists of timber baulks, with a roadway of poles or rough planks, not fastened down except by a few large stones, and a surface of straw and earth on top of all. Traffic soon works this crust loose, and it falls through the interstices of the loose planks, &c.; frequently the crust is wanting, and the corduroy surface works into gaps; but as long as it is possible for a beast or a man to find sufficient foothold, no repair is considered necessary.

At the second river, some eighty yards across, were numerous thrifty Koreans, who, to save the loss of money, and possibly of time (though time is of little value in Korea), involved in taking the ferry-boat, preferred to strip to the waist and wade across. They formed a curious sight with their large black hats, white coats, long pipes, and naked legs. Higher up I saw three or four women also wading across, apart from the men, and from their shorter stature they had on nothing but their "shoulder jackets." The dress of the lower order of native women consists of a very loose pair of trousers or long drawers of native cloth or Manchester shirting, reaching to the ankles, and fastened round the waist by a cord; over this is a petticoat of the same material, reaching to the calf; on the shoulders is a jacket with sleeves, which covers the chest, but is so short that it leaves the breasts exposed to view. This peculiar dress often caused a shock to our feelings by exposing to our view terrible sores on the breasts, sometimes dressed with a blue ointment, but more often neglected. North of Won-san we did not observe nearly so many sores, though the dress still afforded the same facilities for doing so. Girls of a marriageable age (when one sees them, which is not often, as they are kept in seclusion) have a sort of belt round their bodies hiding their breasts. The women plait their hair into tails, which are then wound round the head. Of feminine dress of the higher classes I know nothing, as they are kept carefully secluded from masculine view; and even of the peasantry I saw but very few girls between twelve and sixteen, and those only in the remoter districts. The female Korean to a Western eye is hideous, even in childhood, though the boys are often very handsome, as indeed are a few men. The woman in Korea is merely a useful machine to provide for the wants of the man; marriage is a bargain, and chastity is expected only from the wife; the husband may keep concubines or indulge in others forms of vice, but the wife must be chaste under pain of death; her part is to bear children, to rise early, to get to bed late, to keep the fields, gardens, house, and stables in order, and, in short, to be the woman of all work. What wonder then that amongst the labouring classes they become wrinkled and haglike at an early age? This does not apply to women of the upper class, who, kept in rigid seclusion, do nothing at all, and see no one but their husbands, parents, and female friends. The remarriage of widows is strictly forbidden, which occasionally leads to scandals and the death of the woman. The soil is in general so fertile, and the wants of the Korean are so few, that the male peasant has on an average eight months of the year in which he does nothing but gossip and smoke, while seed-time and harvests fill up the other four months; but women and children are always at work, indoors or out. Koreans lay great stress, as points of beauty, upon the small size of the hands and feet; because, I fancy, showing high-breeding, brought about by long-continued ancestral immunity from manual labour. We did not observe that the mandarins affected the long talons of the Chinese, as evidence of belonging to the intellectual and aristocratic drones, in distinction to the inferior species of man, who is so degraded as to have to do hard work with his hands, and must therefore have short nails. But what we did observe was the scrupulously clean, carefully tended, well-shaped, soft white hands of the Korean swell mandarins; and in contrast we felt most painfully conscious of the size and muscular development, as well as the sunburnt and dirty appearance, of our hands and nails. Do what we could to keep them clean, a short supply of hot water, and much handling of dirty saddlery, guns, Rangoon oil, cartridges, boxes, and packages, with constant exposure to dust, hot sun, and cold winds, rendered our hands terrible sights.

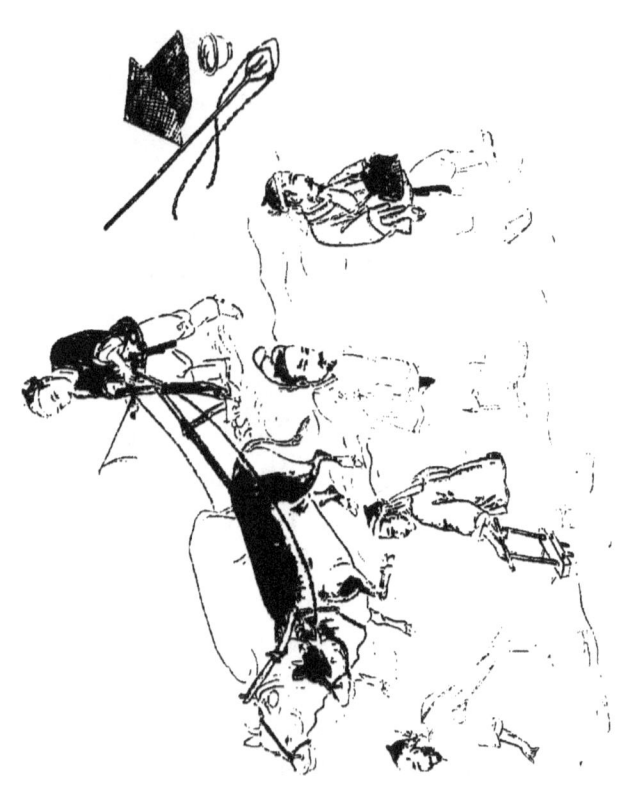

CHAPTER IV.

WON-SAN.

WE have at last reached the native town of Won-san. Being the tenth day of the moon, it was a market-day (for a market is held every fifth day), and buying and selling was in full swing when we entered, causing us considerable difficulty in forcing a passage through the crowd. Having at length got through the town, which contains 15,000 inhabitants, we saw about a mile in front of us European-looking houses, flagstaffs, and a steamer lying in the harbour. Ere long, after fording another river, we came to the Japanese settlement, with neat little wooden houses, roads laid out, and carefully tended gardens, and finally brought up at the custom-house, where we were cordially received by Mr. Brazier, the assistant Customs officer. He told us that Mr. Oiesen, the acting Commissioner, whom I had met before on a voyage to Ceylon, was to start that afternoon on six weeks' leave to Japan, but had placed his house at our disposal. Thither we betook ourselves, and after luncheon (how good the beer was!) we went with Mr. Oisen to call on the Prefect of Tök-wön, who is the Superintendent of Trade. The Yamen, or Magistracy, is close to Mr. Oiesen's house; so, after sending in our Chinese cards, we were ushered in, and presenting our Foreign Office letter, we explained through "Jumbo," the interpreter, what our business was. The Prefect was very civil, and promised to get ponies for us as soon as possible, offering to give us post-ponies, but this we refused, as we wished to pay our way. The posting system is a flagrant instance how the country-people are down-trodden. Along all the important routes posting-stations are established in the villages about ten miles apart, and the "pony-man," generally the head-man of the village, has to provide ponies and lodging for any official or other person who may be provided with a letter authorising him to travel at the public expense; should the traveller bring ponies, then they and the suite have to be accommodated almost free of charge. The ponies are not, as a rule, kept waiting for travellers, but are working in the fields or elsewhere: consequently, on a demand for them, a delay takes place while the required number and their attendants are torn from the harvest-carrying or ploughing of the poverty-stricken villagers. Korean officials pay nothing, I believe; but whenever we were forced to have post-ponies, we paid a certain amount, generally 100 cash a day for each pony, and always for our lodgings, which is apparently customary with European travellers in Korea. Having smoked a cigarette with the genial mandarin, we took our leave and went home to wash and dress. What a luxury it was to get into a comfortable room, a large bath, and clean easy clothes, after eight days of shooting-boots and breeches!

Mr. Oiesen's house was built by his predecessor, in the Korean style, the roof composed of immense beams, morticed

PREFECTURAL YAMEN AT WON-SAN.

into small uprights, with a verandah in front; on one side was a small conservatory, and in front of the house a flower-garden, while behind were the stables and a kitchen-garden. The house stands on the slope of the valley of a little stream, and faces about east by south, the low hill behind and on each side keeping off the bitter north and north-west winds in winter: about twenty yards lower down on the left is the Yamen, and about fifty yards farther, on the right, is Brazier's tiny house, built on a shelf cut out of the hillside; on each side of the stream are vegetable gardens belonging to the Koreans or Japanese, also the live-stock yards of the two Europeans. Oiesen had a stork and a large quantity of geese, ducks, and fowls, while Brazier had a crane, a deer (Muntjac), and a lot of poultry. About fifty yards farther still was a little Japanese house, which, with the stream, has a gruesome tale told about it. When the cholera was pretty bad at the Treaty ports in 1890 (140 Japanese died at Fu-san out of 180 attacked), Oiesen had the Commissioner of Customs from Fu-san with his wife and daughter staying with him. One evening they were all sitting on the verandah, when Oiesen saw some Koreans carry something out of the Yamen down to the stream and begin washing it. He had heard that one of the Prefect's servants had been very ill with cholera in the morning, and now saw that what they were washing was the man's dead body! Hastily making some excuse about dinner being earlier that night, he hurried his guests indoors. Next morning he learnt that the Jap who lived in the little house below was dying of cholera, and then he remembered that the Jap's wife had

WON-SAN, LOOKING EAST-NORTH-EAST.

been cleaning vegetables for her husband's supper in the stream just at the time the corpse was being washed a few yards higher up!

The native town of Won-san is at the southern end of Port Lazaref, and is the great emporium for the east coast and inland trade; beyond it, the plain stretches to the east, ending in the sand-hills on the seashore, and this expanse in winter is the haunt of millions and millions of wildfowl. Here, as in other towns on the coast, one finds for sale, besides the native produce, consisting of straw sandals, hats, wickerwork, fruit, fresh and dried fish, bundles of charcoal, tobacco, cottons and grass-cloth, pipes and cheap trinkets, such foreign goods as Manchester shirtings, German needles, Japanese matches, cheap mirrors, small bottles of dyes, kerosene oil, cigarette papers, and occasionally Japanese cigarettes.

In the foreign settlement we found a store kept by Mr. Ah Sin, an enterprising Chinaman, where we procured some tins of soup and jam, packets of candles, also 50 lbs. of flour, 20 lbs. of sugar, and some other cooking ingredients for which the cook was clamouring. Our biscuits were too full of weevils to eat, and we only took them along with us in case of emergency. To last until the cook could bake some bread-stuff for us, we took some fresh loaves, and had a few others made into toast. Mr. Ah Sin also kept a small hotel, where the tide-waiters of the Customs messed together, though each had built himself a small house, Mr. Knott having two, one for summer and a smaller one for winter habitation.

About 700 Japanese live in the settlement under their Consul, who has a very nice-looking house and offices, built in European-Eastern style; he has some Japanese police under him, armed with rifles and swords; the Japanese also have a bonding warehouse, the office of the Nippon Yusen Kaisha line of steamers, and the post-office. Won-san has a mail by the Japanese steamers *viâ* Nagasaki every fortnight in summer and about once in five weeks in winter; there is also an overland mail from Soŭl by runner occasionally, for official despatches which it would not be safe to send through the Japanese post-office, where I am told that, through the carelessness of the employés, envelopes occasionally become unfastened, and so the contents of letters get known to people not entitled to the information!

The Chinese are about fifty in number, under Mr. Woo, the Consul, who I believe was in England with Marquis Tseng, the ambassador; they also are forming a small police force to act as a check on the Japanese.

Korea is run by the Japanese and Chinese, and it is difficult to say which race the inhabitants hate most; they are, however, more frightened of the Chinese, who always assume superior airs, as belonging to the dominant power. The King of Korea is a vassal of the Emperor of China, but they both rejoice in the title of "King of Heaven." In 1884 there was a kind of revolution in Soŭl, caused by the intrigues of the two factions in the capital, which are the Progressive, urged on by the Japanese, and the Conservative, supported by the Chinese. The Progressives made an attempt to overthrow the Ming family, of whom the Queen is one, all but murdered Ming-Yuen-ik, the Minister (whom we met at Hong-Kong, and who kindly gave us letters of introduction to his relations in Korea), and nearly obtained possession of the palace, but not of the King, who escaped by a back-door. Many lives were lost in this *émeute*, and it ended in the Japanese being forced to fly by night to Chémulpho, and take shelter in a British man-of-war, the burning of their new Consulate, and the triumph of the Chinese Conservative party. Yüan, the Chinese Resident in Soŭl, keeps a body-guard of about 200 soldiers, ostensibly his servants, but they are all trained men, and he has an ample armoury. The Japanese Minister also has a body-guard of about the same strength. In 1887 there was some idea of another similar movement, and the Japanese were detected in the act of smuggling some of their marines and a field-gun into the city. A treaty was made in 1885 between China and Japan, by which neither country can keep an army in Korea, nor can the one land troops without informing the other of the intention beforehand; but this treaty is evaded by both parties keeping up these body-guards and police.

Immediately after breakfast on Sunday morning, we paid off our "mapus," giving them the $15 still owing, but not the extra $1, as we had fined them that for allowing the bottle of whisky to get broken. We now found out why they had taken the most difficult road, for they demanded extra payment because they had been so long on the road! However, they did not get it. The distance by the main road from Soŭl to Won-san is reckoned at 525 li, easily done in good weather in six days, while we had taken $7\frac{1}{2}$ days to do almost the same distance. I had written some time before to Oiesen, asking him to see if he could hire some ponies for us, and telling him when we would leave Soŭl. Finding we did not turn up on the sixth day, he had telegraphed to Soŭl to know if we had left, and the answer that we had done so on September 5th exercised his mind considerably as to the cause of the delay.

The Won-san-Soŭl telegraph goes to Chémulpho, and I believe a submarine cable is being, or has been, laid to Chefoo or Tientsin: a cable already exists from Fu-san to Nagasaki. It is proposed to extend the Soŭl line to Ham-heung and Wladivostock, and we saw the poles lying in heaps by the roadside; but many of them have been removed for firewood, and other heaps have been set on fire through wanton mischief. The telegraph at Won-san is worked by a Korean, the office is in the Yamen, and the English language is employed, as it is at present impossible to signal Chinese symbols!

The hire asked for ponies going to the north was each 130 cash for 10 li, or, reckoning 80 li as a day's march, exchange being 555 to the dollar, nearly two dollars a day. This we would not give, nor would the livery-stable keeper or ponyman come down in his price. However, the Prefect promised to get the hire knocked down a bit, for it appeared that Mr. Woo paid 80 cash for 10 li when travelling, while the Japanese Consul said he had paid as little as 40 cash. Traffic to the north not being great, and the food obtainable being of worse quality, caused the difference in prices, for from Soŭl we had only paid 39 cash; and remembering Grosvenor's story of travel in Western China, we had offered 80 cash for 10 li, but in vain. The story is so thoroughly typical of Chinese and Korean inaccuracy, that I may be pardoned for repeating it. He was told that the distance between two places depended upon which end one started from; thus from A to B might be one mile, while from B to A would be three miles! An intelligent native thus explained this to him. Carriage being based on so many cash per mile, a coolie ought to be paid more if the road were uphill; but as it would be troublesome to adjust the tariff according to the gradient of the road, it is more convenient to assume that, according to the difficulty or precipitousness of the road, the objective is farther off. On Grosvenor urging that, at this rate, wet weather must elongate the road, which would also be longer by night than by day, he was met by the answer, "Very true, but a little extra payment will adjust that!" He found that the scale was about the following:—On level ground, one statute mile equalled 2 li; on ordinary hill-roads, it equalled 5 li; but on very steep roads, it ran as high as 15 li.

On Sunday night Brazier gave a dinner-party, consisting of the Prefect, Mr. Woo, the Japanese Consul, and ourselves; a strange mixture of races at one table, Scotch, Irish, English, Korean, Chinese, and Japanese! The Prefect ate his dinner like a man, and drank of everything, but only one glass of each kind of liquor. He was magnificently dressed in blue and crimson silk robes, with white trousers; from his hat, woven of fine hair, hung a long chain of amber beads which went round his neck. The seals of office, without which an official dare not move, were deposited under his chair by the seal-bearer, a boy of sixteen with a huge pig-tail, round whose waist were slung his master's tobacco-box, spectacle case, and purse. After dinner the Prefect had his long straight-stemmed pipe with amber mouthpiece lighted, and puffed away at some of our tobacco with great appreciation of its strength. Korean tobacco is very mild, and by no means first-class in quality, but the best makes very fair cigarettes. The poorer classes smoke unmanufactured stuff, just the leaves dried in the sun and broken up a little. I was several times given some of the common kind by the natives, and tried to

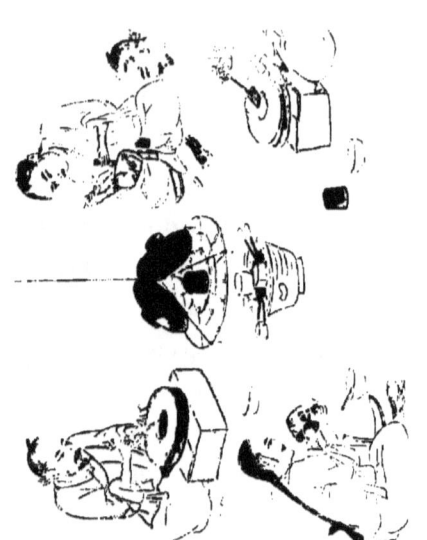

smoke it, but the smoke of burning weeds was quite harmless and pleasant in comparison.

The Prefect's spectacles were about two inches in diameter, made of pebbles, set in a large amber frame, worth altogether about 15 dollars or 7500 cash; officials wear spectacles partly as a protection from dust and glare, &c., but chiefly as a sign of dignity. Another article brought into the dining-room was a round brass pot, the use of which we did not at first comprehend, but afterwards we learnt it was the custom for the guest to bring his own *pot-de-chambre*. The Prefect belongs to a rich family in Soŭl, and lives at Tŏk-wŏn, about three miles to the south-west, and thither he started about 10 P.M. in his chair, accompanied by a dozen or more attendants carrying paper lanterns. His suite includes about seventy "soldiers," who do odd jobs for him and show off his state and dignity. One of these warriors the Prefect kindly said he would send with us, to look after, show the way, and lend an air of importance to our party.

We had a little difficulty about getting money here, as the branch of the first National Bank of Japan was unable to make advances on our letters of credit. The difficulty was solved by our giving cheques on the Hong-Kong and Shanghai Bank to Mr. Hintze and Mr. Knott in the Customs service, in return for 300 Japanese "yen." A hundred of these we turned into cash at 555 to the yen, but even this was not enough for our requirements. According to the Prefect, the "mapus," and "Collected Administrative Regulations" or "Tai-jön-Hoi-thong," a Korean official book, the distance from Won-san to Chang-jin, whither we were bound, was 800 li, whereas we estimated it at 650 li. There is no reliable map of the country, as it has never been surveyed; the best is the Russian staff-map, which is based on the Japanese official one published in 1875, but it contains the same errors, with a few more on its own account. In Soül the Italian Consul showed us an old Korean map on a very large scale, two or three miles to the inch, in eighteen sheets, on which to some extent the Japanese map relies as regards the interior, but the constant trading journeys of the Japanese merchants have corrected much of the erroneous representations of the country. The li, which properly measures about 486 yards, varies greatly, according to the proximity of the capital; the farther one recedes from the "Heart of Korea," the longer grows the li, until in the extreme north and south it measures as much as 555 yards, while in mountainous country it shortens to about 430 yards; consequently it is impossible to form any reliable estimate of the distance between two places until one has travelled the road. The Koreans also are extremely stupid and ignorant about distances, and appear to take no note of the time it takes them to get from one place to another. The Prefect succeeded in knocking down the pony-hire to 110 cash for 10 li per pony, to which we had to agree, but decided to reduce the number of ponies to eight, Goold Adams and I to ride turn about, while the servants and soldier were to walk. The "mapus" demanded an advance of pay for each pony of 7000 cash, or prepayment for 636 li, which we had to give; consequently another twenty yen had to be converted into cash. The currency of the country is copper cash, of which, at the time of our visit, 550 to 560 were equal to a Mexican dollar or Japanese yen; but Soŭl has a currency of its own, consisting of new copper cash, coined in 1890, one of which is, by royal decree, equal to five of the old ones, but intrinsically they are each worth less than one old cash piece, and so brittle that if let fall they often break. The rate at which we exchanged dollars for these in Soŭl was 650 five-cash pieces to one dollar, but these cash were not accepted at Won-san or Fu-san.

The day before leaving Won-san we paraded our ponies, and a sorry sight they were; the galls were too sickening in some cases, and we had to reject two or three animals as quite too bad to go with us.

We heard several stories about tigers and leopards here, for in the winter many of these beasts come down from the mountains to the plains for food. On the An-pyön plain, stretching from the Prefecture of that name to Won-san, they are often caught and killed in traps. In 1890, seven leopard-skins, thirty tiger-skins, and three live tigers were sent away from here by sea; and as evidence of these animals being common in the country, in the same year sixty-seven of these skins were exported from Chémulpho. One winter's night a

A TIGER-TRAP.

tiger passed close under Oiesen's bedroom window and tried to get at Brazier's poultry; another night a tiger seized one of Knott's dogs and carried it off. Knott was aroused, and going out with his gun, saw the thief standing on the hillside just above his house. He tried a charge of AAA at it, but apparently did no harm. Another time Brazier was out shooting just behind the settlement, and encountered a leopard making its way across the plain, but he wisely left it alone. Yet another story. Mr. Woo had some fine geese with a very fierce gander, which he did not very carefully shut up at night, saying the gander was strong enough to take care of itself! Shortly after, a tiger visited his poultry-yard, removed his gander and two geese, devouring them on the hill above his house. He has a native tiger-trap, which consists of a cage made of logs of wood, and firmly fastened together; at one end a space is partitioned off by a strong paling and weighted down with earth and stones, and in this is placed a pig; at the other end is an opening for the tiger or leopard, attracted by the cries of the pig, to enter, and as soon as he is fairly inside, he presses against a string which releases another cord holding up a falling door, which in its descent closes the trap; the animal is unable to turn owing to the narrowness of the trap, cannot get at the pig, nor can he escape, and eventually dies by starvavation or the spear-thrusts of the natives. So destructive of human life are these beasts, that when the natives have to go out to collect brushwood for fuel, they do so in parties, and appoint a rendezvous near the village before separating in the evening. The carriers returning each with an enormous load of fuel, are carefully counted to see if any are missing, having been killed by a wild beast on the mountain-side. In spite of this, whenever we asked about tigers, the natives invariably denied any knowlege of them, as soon as they suspected our wish to go in search of the beasts.

A Russian coasting steamer came in the day before we left, bringing the news that sixteen convicts employed on the Trans-Siberian Railway had escaped, and were murdering people in the neighbourhood of Wladivostock for their clothes and money; a French naval officer, some Chinese and Japanese had already fallen victims, and the inhabitants were in a state of panic, while revolvers were not to be obtained for love or money. We were cautioned that very possibly we might meet some of them working their way down to Won-san. When I returned here later on, I learned that all the fugitives had been captured, after having murdered the bandmaster of the band which played at the funeral of the French officer. Several were hanged, and others sent to the island of Saghalien, to many a more severe punishment than death, as it ranks next to the quicksilver mines in its horrors.

CHAPTER V.

WON-SAN TO CHANG-JIN.

HAVING ordered our ponies to come at 7 A.M. on Tuesday, September 15th, we were glad to see them arrive at 10 A.M. A grey mare about fourteen hands high was produced for us to ride, and after much haggling about the loads, which the "mapus," egged on by our servants, declared were too heavy, we started at 10.20 A.M. We vainly pointed out that in coming from Soŭl eight ponies had carried all our baggage and the three servants, while now seven ponies were to carry the baggage only, or about 400 lbs. less. The real reason for the grumbling was that our servants did not wish to walk, and they took measures to ensure riding without our knowledge, as I shall explain a little later.

Our project now was to go to Chyŏng-phyŏng, thence branch off to Chang-jin, and so to Sam-su on the Yalu, calculating we could do this distance, barring accidents, in fifteen days' travel; then making Sam-su our base, we hoped to get some shooting on the other side of the Yalu in Manchuria, gradually working our way by Hyei-san to Po-chŏn. G.-A. and

I had also become bitten with a desire to ascend the Paik-tu-san or Ever White Mountain, which Captain Younghusband, Mr. Fulford, and Mr. James had ascended in 1887, as described in the latter's book "The Long White Mountain." I had to return to Won-san by the end of October, as I wanted to go to Japan, and had pledged myself to the General commanding at Hong-Kong to make my leave of absence as short as I could, while G.-A. intended to stay in the north, after we should part company, if there was any shooting to be got, returning to Won-san or Soŭl about the end of November, his leave not being up till December 15th.

Before parting from our kind host Brazier, he insisted on G.-A. taking his long sheep-skin coat, which the latter found very warm and comforting, even before I left him; he also gave us four bottles of whisky, and started us off with a basket of beetroots, turnips, and some very fine tomatoes. Mr. Woo had also lent us a "shoe" of silver or a "sycee." This is a useful and more portable way of carrying money than copper-cash; it is an ingot of pure silver, from which pieces can be cut off as required and exchanged for cash; its shape is somewhat like a Chinese shoe, hence its name; its value was about 80 yen, and we subsequently were very glad we had taken it.

We journeyed inland over the plain of rice-fields and past Tök-wön, the Prefectural Yamen, which was approached by an avenue of Scotch firs, 400 yards long. Here we had to ford the river, as the bridge was only now being put up again for the winter. I got over on the mare, while G.-A. crossed on a man's back. We left the cook, the interpreter, and the soldier behind, as they were loitering for a purpose of their own.

This alluvial plain, stretching from the seashore four or five miles inland, continues more or less as far as the Yeung-heung river, cut here and there by low spurs running to the sea. It seemed to us that the granite hills here owed their shape in a great measure to glacial action. Many enormous boulders, grooved and carved in a manner no weather could effect, lay in situations only to be accounted for on this supposition. Moreover, in the centre of this plain, where the foot of the glaciers would have been, we noticed piles of boulders, which we took to be remnants of moraines.

The road was broad and good-going, except where the overflow of a rice-field had turned it into a quagmire, and after passing the village of Ti-kyöng we halted for the night at Mun-chön. After we had pitched our tent on the left bank of the river, G.-A. took his rod, and we strolled up the river for a mile or so. The heat of the day made us long for a bathe, but we could not manage it, there being too many people about, women washing clothes, and boys spearing fish with wooden tridents. The accuracy with which these naked brown imps speared the small fish, which we could see darting about in the clear water, was astounding. We also saw a man carrying a freshly speared salmon, but he refused to sell it, and the river yielded no return for G.-A.'s efforts in angling.

While we were at dinner to-night, the cook produced a "pony-letter," an official document authorising the bearer to be supplied with a certain number of post-ponies. This, he said, had been given to our servants by the Prefect of Tökwön. We guessed there had been some underhand work about this, and accordingly, two days later, from Yeung-heung, sent back a letter to Brazier, asking him to find out the meaning of it. When I returned to Won-san a month later, I found the Prefect thirsting for the blood of our servants. It appeared that our interpreter had dropped behind at the Tök-wön Yamen, obtained access to the Prefect, and *demanded in our names* a pony-letter, saying those we had were not enough. The Prefect not suspecting anything to be wrong, and knowing we were in such a hurry to get on that it was possible we had no time to come ourselves, granted a letter for *three* ponies only, though it was afterwards found the rascals had added two strokes to the character (三) and made it five (五). When G.-A. brought back Yeung and the interpreter later on, the Prefect had cooled down, and did not punish them, as he told me he was going to do.

While walking this afternoon near a clump of rocks, we heard something crying and making a noise, rather like the hoarse miauling of a cat. Investigation showed us on the other side of a broad muddy ditch a wretched frog, caught by the hind-legs by a small snake, which was trying to twist its tail round the grass stems to get a purchase, and pull the frog, which was clinging to the reeds with all the might of its poor little arms, on to dry land. We were forced to leave them to settle the matter themselves, as the ditch was impassable for us, too wide to release the crying victim with our sticks, and for a wonder not a stone small enough to lift was to be seen.

As a result of the forged letter, which unfortunately we could not read, we found, at starting next morning, our train of ponies augmented to thirteen by the addition of five post-ponies. There was a little beast for me about eleven hands high, which was too small to carry me over the small river beyond So-rai-wön. On account of this, and some obscure process of reasoning, a naked Korean was impressed by the soldier, and obliged to carry over the river on his back, not me, but G.-A., whose larger pony I rode over, although G.-A. is two stones heavier than I am.

After stopping 2¼ hours at Ko-wön for luncheon, we passed the Tök-chi river by ferry-boat, and about 4 P.M. a thunderstorm with heavy rain came upon us from the mountains on our left; but this, the only storm we met with on our travels, only lasted half an hour. Crossing two ranges of low hills, one of which separates the two branches of the Yeŭng-heung river, we descended again to the fertile plain, growing rice and millet in profusion, and about six o'clock came to the prefectural town of Yeung-heung, containing about two hundred houses. Just at the entrance and a little way off the road, we found an official building which was intended for use by the archers when practising shooting under the superintendence of the magistrate, and a range of 150 yards long, marked out in front of it by boundary-stones, though at present the ground was under cultivation. Incautiously we selected a bare patch in front of this building for our camping-ground, but regretted it bitterly afterwards, when we found the inhabitants came in swarms, and finding such a convenient shelter as the building afforded, remained for hours watching our movements. However, it made a good kitchen, and sleeping-place for the servants.

We were detained here for a whole day by rain, which lasted well into the next night. Two expeditions to the river in search of game revealed only the sight of three widgeon, two pink ibis (*Ibis Nippon*), specimens of which lovely bird we had seen the day before, a golden oriole, and numerous cranes, storks, and cormorants. However on Friday morning it cleared up, and we were able to resume our journey. Before starting we despatched the letter to Brazier by a runner, who had the impudence to ask him for 5000 cash, which he said we had promised him. As we had requested Brazier in the letter to give the runner a *suitable* reward, he did not accede to the demand.

Leaving at 7.45 A.M., we forded one channel of the river, but were brought up a hundred yards farther on by the main channel, which was deep and running swiftly after the rain. After much shouting, we learnt that the ferry-boat had been removed, and we should have to wait for some considerable time for another. We decided to go round by the ferry lower down, which we had noticed the day before, but the men in charge of the baggage-ponies could not be induced to follow us. Passing through the town again, we got to the ferry just as the boat was pushing off with four fine heavily laden bulls on board, and our soldier forced their owners to disembark them, in spite of my protestations. These the Koreans did not, or would not, understand in the least, for, according to their code of etiquette, because we were travelling with a certain amount of officialism, we, or rather they on our behalf, were entitled to bully the peaceable inhabitants as much as possible. Having safely crossed the stream, we rode up the other bank to the ferry where we had left our baggage-ponies, and found they also had got across, the ferry-boat having been produced shortly after we turned back. Our "mapus" were so angry at having had to go 10 li round, that one of them "went for" the ferryman, who took to his heels, and after an exciting chase eventually escaped.

About 11 A.M. we came to a low range of hills, and on the side of one spur by the roadside we saw an outcrop of graphite; it seemed of good quality, and Yeung informed me it was "all same stuff put in pencil." We now came to the Keum-ha-wön gold-diggings or washings; the valley had a small stream running through it, and the beds of this and its tributary rivulets had been dug up in all directions to a depth of eight or ten feet. In the centre of the valley was a collection of miserable mud-houses, the shelters for the washers, and the road wound about the pits in a very bad state, as it had constantly to be shifted before the advance of the diggers, who, owing to their feeble appliances for keeping out the water, had to abandon their excavations on reaching the above depth. We were told all the gold had been sent away the day before, but a considerable quantity is obtained from this and other washings in the Yeung-heung district. The amount of gold exported in 1889 from the three Treaty ports was valued at $982,091 (about £157,135), of which Won-san, which taps the Phyöng-an province, sent away $543,844 (about £87,000), while in 1890 the total amount was $749,699 (about £120,000), of which Won-san exported $556,904 (about £89,100). Of these amounts China took in those years $373,677 (about £59,800), and

$474,600 (about £76,000), while Japan took $608,414 (about £97,335), and $275,099 (about £44,000). In 1891 the total export of gold was about $690,000 or about £110,400 worth, but it is considered that nearly as much more left without being declared or was smuggled across the borders.

Crossing a pass 600 feet above the sea, we came upon some more gold-washings, which appeared to be nearly worked out; and after being ferried over the Shé-chin river, we came to Ko-san. Here we were baulked in our efforts to avoid the native curiosity, for no sooner had we sat down some distance out of the village to have our lunch, than down came the rain, and we were forced to take shelter in a house. The rain leaving off about 3.30 P.M., enabled us to start with fresh post-ponies, and another stretch of amazingly fertile plain, about ten miles in length, brought us to a small suburb of Chyöng-phyöng, at the junction of the Ham-heung and Chang-jin roads. A large graveyard with Scotch firs was on a slight eminence above the road, and here we pitched our tent. The villagers came in such crowds that we fled to the top of a neighbouring hill, and waited there half-an-hour, in spite of the tormenting mosquitoes. During this time a flock of teal went whistling overhead from the north, but we could not see them in the dark. Returning to the tent, we changed our clothes, for the adult curiosity was engaged with the cooking operations, but the juvenile sightseers kept applying their eyes to every hole and crevice in the tent, varying this by letting go the tent-ropes. However, about eight o'clock they left us in peace. From here we could see the wall of the Governor's Yamen at Ham-heung, on the side of a hill above the town, about 50 li to the E.N.E., while eight miles to the east were the waters of Broughton Bay.

Lured on by the prospect of sport on the Chinese side of the Yalu, we decided to branch off here and go due north to Chang-jin and Sam-su, instead of going round by Ham-heung and Kap-san. The latter place we had been warned to avoid, as Campbell, the Vice-Consul, two years before had a row with the inhabitants and had been stoned by them. Our soldier told us he knew the short road to Chang-jin, and after a considerable amount of difficulty, we induced the pony-men to come the way we wished, and not by Ham-heung. We now found that one of them had only come with us, because he wanted to get to Ham-heung on the "cheap;" so he quietly stopped behind here, though we took on his pony. Passing through the town of Chyöng-phyöng, a place of about 300 houses, rejoicing in a Prefect of the second class, we went up a stream, first to the north and then to the north-east. About 25 li from Chyöng-phyöng we reached some more gold-washings, but there were not many diggers, and the place looked as if it was nearly worked out, as the beds of the streams had been dug up to their sources. Five li farther on we crossed a low range of hills 400 feet above the sea, and came down to the wide Ham-heung plain. Skirting this and the foothills in a general north-west direction along a very good road, at noon we passed the village of Tang-yé, about twenty houses, but our "mapus" said there was no accommodation

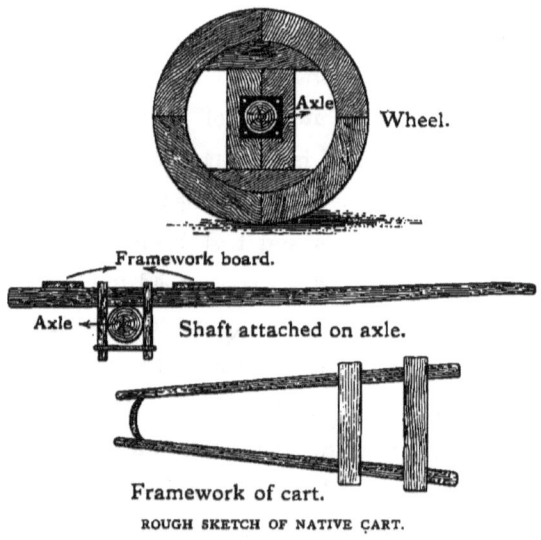

ROUGH SKETCH OF NATIVE CART.

for ponies there, so we went on. All day up till now we had been accompanied by a Korean trader, whose bale of goods was carried by a coolie; he could speak a little English, and by this means and through Yeung, who knew him, we learnt he was on his way from Won-san to Wladivostock by land; he could speak Russian, and had a brother settled there, and came this way to avoid Ham-heung and its officials.

For the first time we saw carts actually in use for carrying the harvest, which was now just commencing about here. The construction of these carts, of which during the day I counted fifty, is simple in the extreme. The circumference of the wheels is divided into four equal arcs, fastened by trenails to cross-pieces; the nave is wedged to the axle, which turns with it; the shafts fit on to the axle by means of two stout pins, fastened by straw rope; the framework consists of two narrow boards, and the ends of the shafts are fastened to a curved yoke, which is tied to the bull's neck by a straw cord.

After crossing several streams, we came about three o'clock to Orichun, a small place of fifteen houses, near the fork of the So-chön river, and on the high-road from Ham-heung to Chang-jin. From here Ham-heung was distant about 45 li, and as we reckoned we had done 70 li to-day, we had saved, by our short cut, 25 li and the delays inevitable had we gone to that town. Little did we dream how much time we should waste by coming this way!

The valley of the river was about five miles wide, and there were three or four stony channels, through which shallow narrow streams now flowed, though we could see that in summer flood these would be full and the width of water increased tenfold. Orichun was protected by an embankment from these floods, and so was Kut-yang, another little village farther up the valley.

We baffled the curiosity of the inhabitants by hanging up towels and waterproof sheets, at the expense of sitting in a very hot tent; but next day rain came on, and we were able to wash and dress with open doors.

The animal produced to-day for my riding was a sturdy little stallion, in better condition than most ponies, but the neighbourhood of G.-A.'s mare was too much for him. If the mare went in front, he pulled my arms off trying to get near her; if she went behind, then he walked as slowly as possible, squealing and yelling all the time. Once or twice when the two met he kicked the mare, narrowly missing G.-A.'s leg; and after a time I got tired of all this trumpeting and fuss, so I walked 60 li out of the 70 we did. In subsequent marches, for he accompanied us to Kap-san, he was relegated to pack duties, and his constant yelling was a valuable guide to the whereabouts of the baggage-train.

A walk along the river to Kut-yang and back in search of game was fruitless, for I saw only a crane, two kingfishers, and a snipe, which got up a hundred yards off. I managed, however, to get a bottle of very good honey here, which formed a welcome addition to our fare, or rather my fare, as G.-A. could not agree with it; so he ate jam and I ate the honey.

H

Next morning at 1 A.M. it began to rain, and a steady downpour continued all day until 8 P.M. G.-A. shot two teal (? Baikal teal), large handsome birds, male and female; steel-blue bodies, wings dark blue lightening to azure blue, with the two longest feathers tipped with 1½ inches of white, breasts white, and beaks scarlet; the male had a chestnut crest, the female's head was steel-blue without a crest. It being impossible to procure eggs or chickens here, we were glad to get a change in our bill of fare. This difficulty about food is one which every traveller in Korea encounters, and it is a moot-point whether it arises from unwillingness to sell or fear of not being paid, on the part of the inhabitants. On the 7th, 8th, 9th, 11th, 15th, 16th, 18th, and to-day we could not obtain any, although we were at such large places as Nam-san, Mun-chön, Yeung-heung, and Chyöng-phyöng, and saw cocks and hens in numbers wandering about, besides being wakened in the morning by the crowing. In Korea, when an official of any rank travels, he and his attendants pay for nothing except their lodging, and by right the persons and property of the inhabitants of the villages are at their disposal. Consequently the visit of an official is a very expensive matter to a small community, and it is perhaps a fortunate thing that it is not part of the duty of the governors and mandarins to make personal inspection of their provinces or districts. Two German travellers arriving at a village in

the Diamond Mountains in the Kang-wŏn province this autumn, found they could not buy any chickens, though there were a great many walking about. On inquiring for the owner of these fowls, every one said they had no owner, so one of them got his gun and shot three; it then turned out they belonged to their landlord, who demanded payment for them, which, in spite of his lies, the Germans made. As in China, lying is in Korea a fine art and a cardinal virtue.

Leaving Orichun at 8 A.M. on September 21, we slowly ascended the river by a very good road for Korea, passing Sam-ba-gon at 25 li, and halting for lunch at Wung-bon-i, a little place of ten houses. Hence we continued our way up the narrowing gorge of the river for some time, till its course trended too much to the west, which obliged us to go over the Chyöng-na-jöng pass, 2050 feet above the sea, and thence we descended 650 feet to the tiny hamlet giving its name to the pass on the right bank of a tributary of the So-chön river. We pitched our tent under two large walnut-trees, which helped to shelter us from the rain which came on at nightfall. The scenery was rather fine; the granite mountains shutting in the river being some 2500 feet in height, and clothed with pines, beeches, maples, and oaks. There being no posting-stations on this road, we brought the five post-ponies with us, as we could not procure others.

The following morning we got off by 7.30, and the thermometer being only 49°, we were glad to walk to keep ourselves warm. After passing the boundary of the Phyöng-an province, which consisted of a ruined stone-wall about two feet high, running from the river up the mountain-side, having a wooden gate like a Japanese "torii," with the crest of the province at each end of the cross-beam, we began to ascend a pass in the Paik-ŭn mountains, which form the watershed of Eastern Korea. In 1½ hours we climbed 2800 feet up a steep forest path, obstructed by fallen trees, mudholes, and boulders, where the only sounds besides those we made were of trickling streams and the rustling of cheeky little grey and white striped squirrels.

I noticed some magnificent beeches three and four feet in diameter, also Scotch firs, pines, oaks, birch, and maple, the latter just beginning to turn red. From the top of the pass we had a fine view down the valley we had come up as far as Broughton Bay, but to the right, left, and behind us the view was restricted by mountains. Korea is so mountainous that it is but very rarely one gets an extensive view in any direction in the interior. On the top of the pass we left the province of Phyöng-an by passing through a narrow gateway in the boundary-wall which ran along the crest of the pass. Descending 200 feet to a small stream flowing to the west, we very shortly had an ascent of 400 feet by a forest path, which was very muddy and at times boggy. From this height we followed an abominably stony track down to Kot-e-su, a dirty village of twelve houses, on the right bank of the Chang-jin river. On the northern side of the pass the change from early to late autumn was most marked; the oaks, beeches, &c., were in their yellow and brown dress, many of their leaves had already fallen, the bracken was brown, while the maples were a blaze of scarlet. A little trickle of water from the top of the pass, the beginning of the Chang-jin river, accompanied us on our left hand, and in five miles it had become a stream fifty yards broad and three or four feet deep. Much wood had been cut down by the inhabitants of the scattered houses we passed, but the young growth on the mountain-sides presented a magnificent sight with its scarlet maples glowing amidst the browns and yellows, the effect being heightened by the dark green of the pines. Here we saw our first crop of Korean oats, and roofs of the houses made of strips of birch bark or thin slats held down by large stones, with the smoke of the "kangs" going all day.

Leaving Kot-e-su after a stay of three hours, we went on along a plain about a mile wide, evidently formed of the debris brought down from the mountains by the river, as we passed several of its former beds. For some 20 li the river flowed on the far side of the plain to our left, but it then crossed towards us and began to spread itself out into a series of bogs and reedy lakes. Shortly after this change of course, we passed some gold-washings, places of small extent, and kept along a path cut in the hillside to Sa-seu, which we reached at 5.30 P.M. All the afternoon we had a cold south wind with heavy showers, and this decided us on venturing to pass the night in a Korean house, as the ground was so wet.

We had espied some duck on a small lake about a mile from Sa-seu, and as soon as we had settled on our night's lodging, I took my gun and went after them. I had to cross a swamp about 200 yards wide by stepping from one tussock of grass to another, and having executed a stalk to within fifteen yards of the unsuspecting duck, I spoilt it then by slipping up to my knees in a hole, the splash of course frightening them away before I recovered foothold enough to fire. Wet, weary, and disgusted I returned to Sa-seu. A liberal use of Keating's powder kept away the fleas, but the room was so heated by the "kang" that we had to sleep with the door open.

From this village in the swamps we pursued our way next day, at first over a plain of the same character as before, but about two hours after starting we crossed over a hill to the north-east, and came down again to the river, which had made a large bend. Soon after this we were ferried over to the left bank at Fut-jen-yé, and had to take shelter there from a smart shower, which delayed us for half an hour. An old man was fishing from the bauk, and we inspected his tackle—a sapling from which dangled about six yards of hemp-line, and the fly consisted of a rusty iron hook with a few deer-hairs and a bit of pheasant-feather. When the weather cleared we went on down the river, the valley becoming more constricted and shut in by hills, 500 feet above it, their sides clothed with vegetation showing the most lovely colouring. From near Fut-jen-yé we saw two mountain peaks about eight miles distant, one to the east and the other to the N.N.E., evidently belonging to the chain of mountains which we subsequently crossed by the Memel-ryöng, and we made their heights to be 6750 feet and 8000 feet above the sea respectively.

We only made a short march, stopping at Sok-chung, because the "mapus" declared there was no other place near. We pitched our tent under a walnut-tree on the river-bank on the only level spot there was, and even then had to stretch our ropes right across the highway, but this did not appear at all strange to any one, and fortunately during the night nothing fell over them. In the evening we walked 5 li down the river looking for game, but saw nothing; here we came to the village of Tjen-ö-su, containing twelve houses, where we might have put up but for the deception of our guides.

Along the crests of the hills on the other bank we noticed snares for birds consisting of a pole with a cross-piece at the top, half-way down a sapling was fastened cross-ways, and the pliant end tied back to the top of the pole by a horse-hair line, knotted in some curious way to catch birds by the feet; a few days later we saw an unfortunate magpie caught in this way by the recoil of the sapling.

A few yards from us some corn-mills groaned a lullaby for us all night; in this country each of these machines has a stream of water to itself, but in Japan there were, as a rule, two, four, or more opposite each other, and the same runlet filled them alternately, thus saving half the waste of time and water-power involved by the Korean method.

This morning, before we started, we witnessed the shoeing of a pony, which happened to be the obstreperous stallion. The "mapus," tying his fore and hind feet together, cast him, then putting a pole through the lashings with one end on the ground he lay there helpless, half on his back, while they cold shod him. This is the invariable method in use, and the shoes are curious things in their way. The hoof is pared but very little, being nearly as hard as flint; the shoe is not fitted to the hoof, and more often than not it is in two pieces, which are very firmly nailed on with long square-headed nails, three on each side. This is economical, for if one half is worn down more than the other, it can be taken off and replaced without removing and wasting the other half.

Another short march on September 24th brought us to Tcuk-sil-töng at 11.30 A.M., when we had to stop for the night, as there was said again to be no halting-place nearer than Chang-jin. From Tjen-ö-su the valley narrowed to the width of the river in flood-time, there just being room for the road between the left bank and the mountain, though sometimes we had to climb over spurs whose precipitous cliffs forbade any attempt at road-making at their feet. Close to Teuk-sil-töng there is one road over the hill to the village for flood-time and another by the river-brink over planks and brushwood hurdles at the foot of the cliff for low water, and the lower road we followed. By the drift-wood in the trees we could see that the river in flood was some 20 feet above its present level, thereby rendering the whole road here impassable.

The magnificence of the colouring of the mountain-sides beggars description; the trees I noticed in varying autumn foliage were maple (several kinds), beech, oak, birch, poplar, Scotch fir, mountain ash, willow, sycamore, crab-apple, wild plum, wild cherry, and walnut. From the number of shrubs, the show of azalea blossom in spring must be very fine in this valley.

Teuk-sil-töng is a little village of fourteen houses on a small spit of land deposited at the junction of the two rivers, the Chang-jin and another whose source we had crossed on the top of the pass in the Paik-un mountains on the 22nd. A rough road on each bank of this river came from the south-west from villages in Phyöng-an province. There were numerous fish-weirs in this stream, and apparently no lack of small trout, judging from the results obtained by several old men, who were fishing with their primitive tackle. In the afternoon we took advantage of the long halt to have a really good wash with *hot* water, a luxury we had not enjoyed since we left Orichun. In the evening we crossed the Chang-jin river in a dug-out, and, guided by a hunter, visited a bean-field about a mile off, where he said there were always deer and pig to be found. Just before we reached it we saw a fallow-deer disappearing over a low hill out of shot, having seen us too soon, and this was the only result of the expedition, on which Yeung accompanied us, armed with the cook's Japanese sword, though what he expected to do with this weapon we could not make out. During the day we had noticed some very pretty dark blue kingfishers and large flocks of light blue jays with white waistcoats, but the latter seemed to affect places where there were ash and willow-trees in abundance. I was much struck with the beauty and variety of the dragon-flies; with plain wings, there were green, gold, dark blue and dark red flies, while with black tips to their wings I saw scarlet, brown, blue, yellow and purple ones.

At Won-san, before starting, one of our "mapus" had complained of sickness arising from a congested liver, and we gave him relief with three Cockle's pills. To-night he came again, saying he was very bad and felt very cold. Having first given him a strong mixture of essence of ginger and whisky to warm the cockles of his heart, we administered three Cockle's pills, and in a day or two he was fit again. Like most uncivilised people, the Koreans have great faith in the medicinal skill of the white man, but they like their remedies strong. Some days later a Korean came to me to heal his eye, which was much inflamed, and he was much offended and puzzled when I told him to wash and bathe his eye well with *hot* water, and tie a bandage over it to keep the cold out, the only disease being a cold in it. To appease him, after he had washed it well, I gave him a weak solution of whisky and water to bathe it with, which produced just enough smarting to satisfy him, and if it did no good, it did his eye no harm. Their own remedies are rather startling, I believe, like the Chinese, who apply a counter-irritant in an opposite part in most diseases, and in fever they burn the neck and throat with a hot iron. Other medical performances of ours consisted in recommending cleanliness, and in applying carbolic oil to cut heads and limbs of men, and sore backs of beasts.

Next morning, leaving at 8.15 in a thick mist, we crossed the tributary river by a curious bridge, 42 yards long, made in three bays; the road-bearers were spars about 36 feet long, and tapering from 2 feet to 6 inches in diameter; these rested on cross-beams wedged and bolted to a single pile, having a long tie upstream. The roadway consisted of small spars laid on loosely, and here and there kept in position by large stones. A similar bridge, of four bays, gave access to Chang-jin.

About 5 li from Teuk-sil-töng we came to a small village

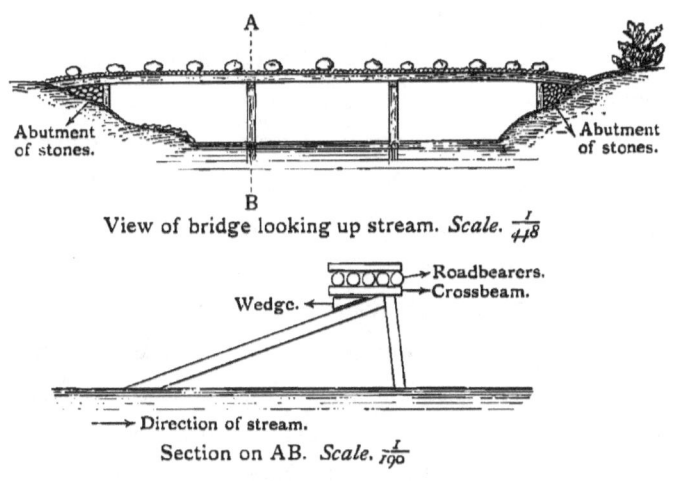

ROUGH SKETCH OF BRIDGE AT TEUK-SIL-TÖNG.

on the right bank of a small river flowing into the main stream from the west, and after another 35 li of rough work, having had three times to cross over hills 200 feet above the river, and at other times make our way along a track overhanging it, and over planks spanning spaces between projecting buttresses of rock, we turned north-west up another affluent of the Chang-jin river, which now took an E.N.E. direction. Fifteen li in this new direction brought us at 2.30 P.M. to Chang-jin on the left bank of the stream, at its junction with another stream coming from the south-west, along which goes the Chang-gé high-road.

In the valley near Chang-jin a young woman came along a path at right angles to the one we were pursuing, and, in spite of the shouts of the "mapus," passed in front of us, which caused a volley of abuse to be hurled at her. We were then told that it is very unlucky for a woman to cross one's path in Korea; which shows that the country is not unlike other countries in some ways. We also saw here a hideous old hag, naked to the waist, working in the fields, and by far the ugliest woman we met in this country of ugly women.

Chang-jin is a town of 300 houses, governed by a Prefect of the second class, and is situated on a small plain at the junction of the river; all round the mountains rise 1000 feet and more above it. As we required both cash to pay our "mapus," and fresh post-ponies to replace the five we had brought from Chyŏng-phyŏng, we sent our cards early in the afternoon to the Prefect, and about 5 P.M. started to pay our official visit. Meanwhile we had been trying to come to terms with our "mapus," and induce them to come on to Sam-su with us; the latter they agreed to, but regarding the money, we were hopelessly at variance. Having at Won-san estimated the distance at 800 li, they now called it 700 li; we, who had estimated it at 670 li, found it to be 550, but we had been stopped two days by rain, which made them two days' food out of pocket, so we allowed for 570 li. Ultimately the Prefect decided we should pay for 590 li; which made 6490 cash to each pony, but having already paid them 7000, the "mapus" now owed us 610 cash on each pony, which they said they could not pay. The difficulty was got over eventually by a further advance of 10,000 cash, which, with the balance, made 1760 for eight ponies, or prepayment for 160 li (8 × 510 = 4080, add 10,000 = 14,080, divide by 8 = 1760, divide by 11 cash per li = 160 li); in addition, the cook's bill against us came to 8818 cash.

We walked through the main street of the town to the Yamen, preceded by our soldier and followed by Yeung, the interpreter, and most of the male population; the large gates were thrown open for us, and after crossing the courtyard, we were ushered into a very dirty little side-room, where the "pusa" was squatting on the floor; there being no chairs, we had to do the same. On the way to call, we had met his present of fresh venison and two chickens coming for us, and, after thanking him for these, and inquiries about his health, we asked him for money and ponies, both of which he promised should be ready the next morning. We were told that the road to Sam-su, only 120 li distant, was very bad, had no stabling on it (this was not true), and we must go round by Kap-san, distant from Chang-jin between 270 and 390 li, according to the varying estimates. With a promise from this civil old gentleman, whose name was Kwo-i-sung, to call on us next day, we returned to our camp by the river, about 150 yards from the town, under a very fine walnut tree measuring 3½ feet in diameter five feet above the ground. Till after eight we were besieged by curious sightseers, to whom a white man was a rarity, and a tent a complete novelty. Mr. Carles was here with our cook in 1884, but the people told us no other white man had ever visited the place.

Next morning, at a little after seven, we heard the trumpets and singing of the Yamen runners, and found the "pusa" was coming to see us. As we were not dressed, we had to send him a request that he would defer his visit to a little later in the day. About 11 A.M. he came again in his state-chair, which was covered with a leopard-skin, and sat down (with care) in one of our chairs in the tent. We gave him a cheroot, and some whisky and water; both before and after drinking he eructated long and loudly, in accordance with the code of Korean etiquette. He promised to lend us 10,000 cash, on the strength of the Foreign Office letter we had, by our giving him I.O.U.'s to be paid through the Governor of the province at Ham-heung, and also four ponies, but the latter he had to get in from some distance, which would detain us till the next day. Making the best of this delay, we then asked him about game, and his answers ran as follows :—" Oh, yes! there were tigers. One lived on the top of a mountain on the north side of the river; yes, some of his hunters had seen it lately. His hunters could not say when they had seen it, and could not point out the place. He would give us men to beat for the tigers. On second thoughts, we had better beat for deer, as his hunters were afraid to encounter a tiger," &c. &c. His suggestion to have a deer-drive in the afternoon delighted us, in the absence of anything more exciting, and gratefully accepting it, we sent him off again, while we had our luncheon in peace. What a drive it was! Outside the town we were met by six hunters with "tiger-guns;" one of whom had a new one (there is a manufactory of these here), which he tried then and there by firing across the river in the direction of the town at a stone about a foot in diameter, which lay at the water's edge at a distance of sixty yards, and, amidst exclamations of admiration of his skill, he hit the mark. The "tiger-gun" consists of an iron tube bound by brass bands to a kind of wooden stock, which is not really a stock, but merely a sort of pistol-handle; there are no sights, and these weapons are discharged by means of a flint-lock, and when firing may be expected, the hunter keeps a slow match burning to ensure ignition of the priming should the flint-lock fail to act, as it frequently does. From the inferior quality of the powder, one is not surprised at the natives being generally unskilful in the use of firearms. "Tiger-guns" are so named, not because they are intended to shoot tigers with—in fact, that is the last animal the owners would wish to face—but because they are such powerful weapons, the tiger in Korea being the emblem of strength. One gun-stock had the brass base of a twelve-bore Ely central-fire cartridge let into it as an ornament; the bullet-pouch is often the skin of the head of a crane, the beak being kept closed by a ring till a bullet is wanted.

Climbing a thousand feet up the mountain above the Changgé road, we were posted some distance apart, and, after waiting half-an-hour, we saw the Prefect come out in his chair and take up a position to watch the sport in a field in the valley below. As I had seen quite fresh tracks of deer leading into a large patch of thin wood between us and the town, we anticipated at least the sight of an animal. Now began the beating of a gong and the blowing of the Yamen trumpet in the direction of the wood, and the two performers on these instruments constituted the beaters, though they did not enter the wood. After waiting two hours in vain, we were told the drive was over, and we gladly returned home to dinner. Thanks to the Prefect, our diet was quite varied here, and we now did better in the way of food than at any other time of our travels, though we always had enough to eat. Here is our bill of fare for the 26th and 27th :—Breakfast: eggs, sausages or grilled chicken, honey, jam, cocoa and milk, or coffee and milk; luncheon: hard-boiled eggs, corned beef or grilled chicken, honey, jam, lime-juice and water; dinner: soup, fresh salmon, venison, preserved vegetables, roast pheasant (shot at Teuk-sil-töng), poached eggs; whisky and water and tea before we went to bed. The salmon had been caught in the Chang-jin river and was perfectly fresh, which shows that this fish is found on the west coast of Korea; although it was a red fish, it was good eating by way of a change.

On Sunday morning, the Prefect having changed his mind about the money, probably fearing that much of his 10,000 cash would be absorbed in passing through Ham-heung before it reached him, sent us 10,600 cash for 20 yen, and Yeung having changed 13 yen for 6730 cash, we were fairly well off. The Prefect sent us a bottle of honey, but it was not so good as what we had before; the only return we could make for his presents was a bottle of brandy and five Manilla cheroots, which he was pleased to accept.

CHAPTER VI.

CHANG-JIN TO KAP-SAN.

IT rained so hard during Saturday night, and so gloomy was it on Sunday morning, that we feared we should lose another day; but about 10 A.M. it cleared up a bit, and we sent for the ponies. Our disgust was great when, instead of the fresh ponies for which we had been waiting, we found four out of the five we had brought with us, and which we had been told must go back to Chyöng-phyöng, and this after the Prefect having said he had obtained three fresh ones for us from the fields, and a fourth which he had to send 10 li for!

However, we got off at 11.15 A.M., and then found we had to go back as far as Tjen-ö-su before branching off to Kap-san. In by no means good tempers we pursued our way back to Tcuk-sil-töng, where we encamped for the night. Our hunter friend met us, and made himself useful in many ways. I can hardly think the 100 cash and four drams of powder which we had given him before was the only reason for his civility, so I put it down in a great measure to the national good-temper. He told us a large black bear had been seen on the hill across the river north-west of the village on the night of the 25th, and the men watching the crops there had had some difficulty in driving it away with fires and torches. We saw many tracks of wild pig here, and were told they were a great nuisance amongst the crops.

Once more saying farewell to Teuk-sil-töng, we arrived at Tjen-ö-su between 9 and 10 A.M. on September 28, having seen many wild duck, widgeon, and wood-pigeons on the way, and after a meal of hard-boiled eggs and venison, we were ferried over the river, and travelled north-east up one of its small tributaries till we came to the Memel-ryöng (pass), passing a small inn 20 li from Tjen-ö-su. Just by the ferry there was a magnificent poplar, 6½ feet in diameter at a height of five feet from the ground, standing solitary in the valley. While waiting for our ponies to catch us up, we met an old man fishing for trout, who, with his primitive tackle, had killed three weighing about 1½ lbs. When, by signs, we asked to see his catch, he was at first much alarmed, thinking we wanted to take them from him, but our friendly manner, I suppose, dispersed his fears, and he exhibited the fish with some pride.

Before reaching the pass we met a marriage procession, apparently the newly-married couple going to the house of the bridegroom's father; the bride, dressed in bright coloured silks with brilliantly painted face, was carried in a chair, while her friend or bride's-maid, almost equally gorgeously attired,

bestrode a miserable pony; about twenty Koreans in clean white suits of Manchester cotton escorted them.

As we began to ascend the pass, we got into the forest again, though the greater part of it had been burnt at no very remote date, but there were still uninjured some large Scotch firs and beeches two to three feet in diameter; the rest of the forest was a young growth of pines, birch, beech, black alder, poplar, and a few maples. Some of the fallen trunks, which, rotting away, covered the mountain-side in hundreds, were of very great size. At the top of the pass, 5300 feet above the sea, there was a small joss-house, and our atttendants duly paid reverence to the Spirit of the Mountain, some by bowing, some by spitting. The silence in this elevated forest was only broken by the rustling of the cheeky little squirrels, who showed no fear of us at all. Up here large quantities of stag's-horn moss carpeted the ground. The road down the east side, through what had once been a fine forest, but was now chiefly bare, charred poles, and young growth five years old, was quite horrible; it was composed of boulders piled one on top of another, and the whole partially submerged in bog. Wherever possible, a deviation from the path (!) into the forest was made, but the spongy soil, fallen trees, and interlacing branches did not often allow the baggage-animals to do this, and we hurried on to avoid seeing, as we expected, the destruction of our property by the falling of the ponies. Our relief was great when, at the end of the march, no damage was reported. The sureness of foot of a Korean pony is something marvellous. Assisting at the birth of a tiny rivulet at a height of 5000 feet, we followed it E.S.E. down a narrow stony valley, till, about 5 P.M., we reached Sul-mul, at its junction with a larger stream called the Sha-phyöng, flowing to the north-east, having on our way passed another small inn at the foot of the pass, 40 li from Tjen-ö-su. Sul-mul is quite a small place of eight houses, and we had some difficulty in finding a level place for the tent, but at last we occupied the threshing-floor of the village. "Sul" means wine, and "mul" means water, but I do not imagine these meanings were attached to the name of the village. The wind was from the north, and very cold, which accounted, I expect, for a large fire lighted by our servants outside the tent, though they said it was to frighten away the tigers; to further keep out the cold they piled oat-sheaves round the tent.

After leaving the Ham-heung plain, the cultivation of rice had ceased, and at these altitudes beans, barley, oats, millet, and potatoes of poor quality were the chief products of the stony fields; chillies and pumpkins were in profusion, and occasionally we saw su-su and tobacco.

The thermometer marked 41° when we started at 6 A.M. next morning, and before we had time to get warm by walking, we had to be ferried over the river, 2 li farther on;

ㄹ호례초날신부신

this operation, as the ferry-boat was composed simply of two dug-outs tied together, involved unloading the ponies and a delay of twenty-five minutes. Whilst waiting on the other side for the ponies, an old Korean cross-questioned us as to our business, thinking we were Chinamen, as no "white man" had ever been this way. He was much struck with our short wooden pipes, out of which he wanted a whiff, but the sight of his mouth and its green fangs made us obdurate. However, he told us the river Sha-phyöng, which now ran north, joined the Yalu, or Amnok, as the Koreans call it. We slowly ascended the bank of a small stream to the north-east till we got to another pass, the Sorin-ryöng, which was crossed at 10 A.M. On the summit, 5770 feet above sea-level, was another small joss-house, also a wooden post showing that here was the boundary of the Kap-san district. One or two of our "mapus" deposited a cash each in the joss-house, and we were told that any offering was sufficient to appease the Spirit of the Mountain—a piece of rag, or even a stone. All the offerings can be taken by passers-by, and generally small boys from the nearest house visit the shrine occasionally to see if there is anything to pick up. Here again we found abundant traces of forest fires, for the mountain-sides looked quite melancholy, all bristling with the white and black skeletons of trees.

After admiring a very fine solar halo, we went down 900

feet by a bad path to Tong-kol-at, a village of ten houses, where we halted two hours for luncheon. G.-A. and I started off again at 3 P.M., and walked till 4.30 P.M. along an exceedingly rough path in the Ho-chhön river valley, which here and there became wide enough for a small field of oats or potatoes. We then sat down, and had to wait forty minutes for the ponies, the lazy "mapus" having made a midday halt of 3½ hours; but the lateness of the hour at which they got in, and their fright in travelling after dark, formed a fitting punishment for them. Clambering along the mountain-side, at times 50 to 100 feet above the stream, with a perpendicular cliff above and below us, and a narrow slippery path beneath our feet, we held on until 6.30 P.M., when we came to a clearing with a couple of huts, which looked so uninviting, and were besides destitute of stabling, that we decided to push on to a better place, which the inmates of the wretched shanties told us was 7 li farther. When we had done this 7 li, we crossed the river by a rough bridge, finding a couple of huts, but no stabling, and were told the place we wanted was only 3 li farther. As it was now quite dark, we got torches and walked on, leaving the soldier to procure more torches and bring on the baggage-ponies when they came up. Stumbling over rocks and clambering along the river-bank, we went on and on, the 3 li lengthening into 10, until, at 7.30 P.M., we got to Sesidong. The instant we lighted on this place, our guide with the torch bolted home, for fear we should chastise him for telling us lies about the distance. We were glad to get into a house and sit by the fire in the smoky kitchen till the others came in about an hour later. A solemn-faced old man sat staring at us, but nothing could rouse him from his stolid apathy; two women, one of them young with a finely developed figure, a girl of six and a baby, completed the party. The old man gave us his room, but there being no door between it and the kitchen, the smells were pretty bad, and the prying eyes of men, women, and children rather embarrassing; fleas and bugs too were plentiful. In small hamlets like this, the kitchen is also the stable, and the inmates of the house, as well as the "mapus," sleep on the "kang" in the kitchen. Slumber is rather disturbed by the jabbering, spitting, coughing, &c., which goes on for hours, and by the stamping, kicking, squealing, and fighting of the ponies.

A Korean is destitute of a pocket-handkerchief, even a paper one, and is not troubled by many scruples on the score of decency or modesty; consequently the various gaseous and more solid excreta of the human animal of both sexes are parted with in the most convenient and *dégagé* manner possible.

Snakes appear to be plentiful, for I had killed a brown adder every day since leaving Chyöng-phyöng. The natives do not kill them, a sort of reverence for these reptiles, probably a relic of serpent-worship, restraining them, but they did not in the least object to our doing so.

A sharp frost at night was followed by a brilliant day, but, after our late hours, we did not leave Sesidong until 8.30 A.M. As we went down the valley, we were surprised to see the extent to which the hillsides here were cultivated; wherever the slope permitted it, a crop of some kind was growing, and I should say the community of Sesidong, living in thirty-four houses, spread along the valley over a distance of 10 li, had at least 500 acres under cultivation. The crops were poor certainly, and consisted of oats, barley, millet, beans, and potatoes. At the end of the village we found a quantity of blue rock pigeons, which had made their home in the cliff, and we secured a couple of them. Later in the day we got some teal and a couple of wild duck, and to retrieve the latter, one of the "mapus" stripped himself naked and waded the ice-cold river. We also wounded a goose, but No. 5 shot at eighty yards did not do it much damage, and it got away before we could get across to it. We lunched at Yangari, a little village in the valley of a small, shallow, and stony river joining the Ho-chhön, which we had crossed and left shortly before; in this valley is grown a good deal of tobacco, which is sent down to the towns in Phyöng-an and on the east coast; every house had strings of leaves drying in the yard formed by the stockade of poles, eight feet high, which surrounded it as a protection against wild beasts, &c. Through this village runs what is called a "small road" from Kap-san to Ham-heung.

From here we crossed a pass 800 feet high, which was called a short cut, as the Ho-chhön river pursued a north-east course and made a sharp bend, till we struck it again and crossed to its left bank about 20 li from Neun-gwi, where we arrived at 5.30 P.M. We put up for the night in a sort of official rest-house, each of us having a small room, with clean matting, but no lack of parasites.

The river here rather puzzled us by flowing to the south-east, but we found next day that it turned again to the north. We were now on the high-road from Kap-san to Puk-chong, and naturally expected to find a better track, but were doomed to disappointment, though the roads were being improved by the sleds, which were being used for carrying the harvest, and also the fuel for winter consumption in the "kangs."

October 1st.—A sharp frost in the night increased our anxiety to get nearer the "White Mountain," and we succeeded in getting the shivering "mapus" to start soon after 7 A.M. Crossing a pass 500 feet high, with one bad boggy place in the ascent, we came down to the stony valley of a small river, which we followed in a north-easterly direction to Ho-rin-cham, where we tried to change ponies, but could not, as there were none in the post-house. Past a small hamlet of six or seven houses, where the "mapus" wanted to stop for luncheon instead of going straight to Kap-san, we hurried on till, at 11 A.M., we again struck the Ho-chhön. Along this stream, now 40 to 80 yards broad, we pursued our way on a road at times positively good, but mostly infamously bad, till, after climbing 200 feet over a projecting cliff, we came to a ferry which transported us to the right bank. Three li farther on, between the river and a small village, was a grove of very fine poplar and willow-trees, which were of course in process of destruction for firewood.

On the other side of a cliff, which, jutting out into the stream, formed a small bay, while the full force of the current striking against it caused a whirlpool in midstream, the valley opened out on both banks; the ground at the foot of the mountains, sloping at an angle of 5° for about a mile on each bank, was chiefly volcanic dust, with many blocks of lava and tuff. The mountains shutting in the valley were of granite and liberally sprinkled with blocks of lava. Close to Kap-san, which we reached at 3 P.M., the road ran through a thick deposit of ironstone by the river-side. We had sent on our soldier, and he got us put up at an official building, a single-roomed house, in which lived one of the Yamen secretaries. By the side of this, raised two feet above the ground on a platform of lava blocks, was an open shed, which appeared to be a storeroom for spears, pikes, &c., used in processions. We did not venture to pitch the tent, owing to the curiosity of the inhabitants; so we accepted the use of the house, which was very dirty and swarming with bugs. The inhabitants came in shoals to gaze at us, and we were forced to close both doors, though the heat of the sun and the "kang" made the room suffocatingly hot.

About five o'clock, having previously exchanged cards with the Prefect, we proceeded to call on him, and this time the big gates were not opened for us. He received us, seated on a black wood stool, over which was thrown a leopard-skin; for G.-A., a chair of black wood was produced, and a stool for me. Beneath each of our seats was a leopard-skin, one a magnificent specimen in the way of winter fur, except that it was rather spoilt by the paws, ears, and whiskers being cut off, and the face trimmed round. The Prefect, in response to our requests for ponies and copper cash, promised the former, but declined to give us any of the latter. As our "mapus" would not take Japanese yen, and we owed them over 20,000 cash, besides having to pay our way to Po-chön and back, it was absolutely necessary for us to get cash. The exchange for yen in the town we found to be 450 cash, and for sycee 475 cash to the dollar or yen; but as this was too much of a "squeeze," we sent Yeung after dinner to the Prefect with Mr. Woo's "shoe," with a request that he would kindly endeavour to sell it for us at a better price, otherwise we could not pay anybody or for anything. Yeung returned with the welcome news that the Prefect would get a reasonable price for us, but that he himself had no money, as he had only been a year in the place, and in that time he had rebuilt the city wall and part of the Yamen, which had exhausted his resources. The unusually neat appearance of the city wall bore out his statement.

Kap-san appeared to be miserably poor, with 300 or 400 houses inhabited, but others deserted and in ruins; the town was much cleaner than Soŭl, and the whitewashed wall surrounding it gave it quite a smart appearance. The district round about is full of minerals of various kinds, gold, silver, lead, and copper; but the appliances for working the mines are so primitive and clumsy that only a bare living can be obtained by the miners, the cost of transport to the coast further handicapping any mineral trade.

About ten o'clock next morning the Prefect came to call, and as he crossed the threshold his satellites shouted something, no doubt laudatory of his "Pusaship," then, following his example of kicking off his shoes, they proceeded to fill the room. We gave him a cheroot, but the poor man had something wrong with his internal arrangements, and, after a puff or two, handed it to an attendant to be kept for a future and more auspicious occasion; he did not, however, object to a

stiff dose of whisky and water. The Prefect, whose name was Hang Nan Yeung, came from Soül, and told us he lived only for the time when he could get back there; his nominal salary was 9000 cash a month, or about £20 a year; but then he lived at the expense of his district, the inhabitants supplying him with all the necessaries of life. He had in his suite two good-looking boys of eighteen, who had magnificent queues of black hair, which we admired, but learnt that their size was due to false hair plaited in. A Korean, until he becomes engaged to be married, wears his hair in a pigtail, without any head-covering, but after that important occasion, which takes place as early in life as his parents can conveniently arrange for, he has his head partly shaved and his hair twisted up into a knot on the top of his head, and can wear one of the numerous hats for masculine adornment. One of our "mapus" discharged at Kap-san was an unattached bachelor, and, although forty years of age, wore a boy's pigtail. On the other hand, we saw several children of nine or ten years of age wearing the marriage top-knot.

CHAPTER VII.

KAP-SAN TO PO-CHÖN.

WE decided to lighten our loads and leave some things in the magistrate's charge, thereby being able to get on with nine ponies, of which only two were hired. Owing to the civility of the Prefect, we got 41,000 cash for the "sycee," or a rate of 512½ cash to the dollar, and we were enabled to get away by 2.30 P.M., accompanied by a soldier of Kap-san, who was to act as guide, the Tök-wön warrior leaving us here without any warning, because, as we afterwards found out, he did not get on with our rascally servants.

A short way from Kap-san we for the first time came upon a fenced-in graveyard, having some carved images surrounding the grave; in this district too we saw several tiger-traps, but all were falling to pieces, the poverty of the inhabitants probably preventing them from risking a live bait. For two hours we kept along the Ho-chhön river in a N.N.W. direction, till it trended W.N.W., when we left it to follow up a tributary coming from the north-east. By 6 P.M. we got to Tong-in, and had to put up in a tiny hot and stinking room, as we had left the tent at Kap-san. G.-A. had left his bed there also, and slept on the floor, where again he was the prey of many creeping things.

We had become tired of the annoyances and delays caused by our hired "mapus," so we paid most of them off at Kap-san, giving them 20,240 cash. Since one dollar's worth of cash weighs about 5 lbs., to lighten our loads we left behind a package of 7000 cash, two magazines, the box of biscuits, and a rifle, and we also forced the cook to leave behind his large box weighing 90 lbs., his canvas valise, weight 60 lbs., and his large kit bag, chiefly full of old shoes and bottles, weight 35 lbs.; all these things were put in charge of one of the Yamen secretaries.

A short time after leaving Tong-in, the following day, while walking on to keep ourselves warm, we met a cow drawing a wooden sled, in charge of a native; the animal, after staring for a few seconds at us, was so alarmed at two such strange beings, that she bolted over the precipitous bank down to and through the river, losing both sled and harness *en route;* on the far bank she stopped, and we left her gazing fixedly at us, while her irate conductor reproached her in the choicest Korean Billingsgate. We had a stiff pull up the An-kang pass, 4250 feet above the sea, and the steep road down the north side was perfectly awful, the slate strata sticking out in sharp edges and jagged points. The view from the top of the

K

pass, where there was a cluster of huts, down the valley towards Un-chong was a peculiar one, the hillsides being cultivated wherever the soil would stand without slipping, and the chessboard appearance made it look like a distant bird's-eye view of the Midlands of England.

Our course was now north-east along a stream, which 15 li farther on turned north-west to join the Ho-chhön river. Arriving at Un-chong at 11 A.M., the head-man of the village, who also hailed from Soül, invited us to his house and to dinner, but the latter part of his invitation we refused. Two villainous-looking Chinamen, probably smugglers of gold over the northern border, came in and watched us while we ate our luncheon. There are about thirty Chinamen here, the biggest blackguards possible in appearance, and we understood they were soldiers discharged from the Manchurian army and now getting a scanty living by trading, gold-digging, and smuggling. Some of these gentry in 1890 robbed and murdered a Korean, and Mr. Woo had to come up here, and, after investigation, deported about twenty of them. The head-man had a silver-handled knife and fork in a silver case of Hamheung workmanship, which he carried slung to his girdle, and in a little bag in his purse he had five or six ounces of gold, probably obtained from the washings here, though he denied having obtained any of it in the district. He produced some samshu, a muddy fluid, which smelt and

tasted like Kaffir beer, with strong spirit in it; this peculiar taste is due to the bean-water which they mix with the spirit distilled from rice or millet. We were given a bottle of this liquor by the head-man, and the cook bought another of Chinese make, which was quite clear and less diluted with bean-water.

After a halt of two hours here, we walked on, and were about to cross the stream by a bridge, when a Korean told us the road lay up the left bank, so we strolled slowly on, inspecting the gold-washing carried on in numerous excavations in the slate, which formed the floor of the valley, a stream of water being turned on to the heap of debris to wash it, but there did not seem to be much gold. We tried in vain to find a place where we could sit down in peace, but as soon as we stopped we were surrounded by half-a-dozen or more Koreans, asking many questions, which we could not answer, examining our clothes, hair, &c., till, wearied by their attentions, we had to move on. While wandering about, we came upon a Korean who had got a pheasant by hawking; the natives are very fond of this pastime, and the bird used is, I believe, a kestrel, which returns to its master after striking its quarry, while the owner's dog retrieves the pheasant. So persistently are these birds hawked, that it is very difficult to get them to rise, for they prefer to run like hares. Near Un-chong there were many tracks leading in all directions, and we were told that numbers of cattle came through here from Phyöng-an on their way to Wladivostock, for the troops in the Ussuri region; large quantities of oats also are exported by land and sea from the northern provinces for the Russian troops.

When Yeung caught us up at 3 P.M. with the ponies, 5 li from Un-chong, having only started at 2.30 P.M., he told us we had taken the wrong road, and that the cook was going with the baggage by the right one. The soldier professed to know a shorter way back to the main road than by going back to Un-chong, but this way involved going 20 li round up the stream, which we crossed by a bridge formed of magnificent spars two or three feet thick, supported on two-legged trestles, and climbing 1000 feet up and down a pass, where we became separated from Yeung and the interpreter, but fortunately picked them up an hour later. Just at dusk we found our baggage-train had halted for the night at a dirty little house 20 li from Po-chön; there being no stables and no room for ourselves, we loaded up again, and procuring torches, started for Po-chön, where we arrived at 9.30 P.M. There was great reluctance amongst our "mapus" to going on after dark, for these forests are said to be infested with tigers, and not free from Chinese bandits; but as they had chosen to stop four hours at Un-chong, we insisted on going on. The road wound up and down over ridges, through a thick forest, and was pretty good going now, but in wet weather it must be a quagmire, for half of it was a corduroy track. It was a fine sight to look back on our long line of torches winding through the silent forest. Our guides, on nearing every settler's house, uttered loud and prolonged shouts of "Hurrl iri onera—bring lights here," as a warning to bring out more torches. These are of birch-bark, or a fir pole beaten and split like a very coarse birch broom, and are a fruitful source of forest fires.

SETTLER'S HUT NEAR UN-CHONG.

It is a regular custom of the country for parties travelling at night to requisition torches from every hamlet and village passed, and the inhabitants light one's path without any thought of remuneration. We tried at first to pay for this service, but found it impossible, as the torch-bearers disappeared into the darkness the instant fresh lights appeared. We stopped for a few minutes to collect the party in what must once have been a frontier-post (judging from its surrounding parapet and official gate), containing a couple of huts occupied by some wicked-looking Chinamen, who absolutely declined to help us in any way. In former days these little forts were erected all along the Chinese frontier, but are now in ruins. It was amusing to see these Chinamen taking stock of the interpreter, and trying to make out what he was, for, unlike the cook, he did not greet them kindly.

At Po-chön we again put up in the head-man's house, which contained two rooms and a kitchen. After dining at 11 P.M., and asking for bearers to carry our impedimenta to the "White Mountains," we were very glad to get to bed by midnight. The head-man asked our permission to leave his boxes in one of our rooms, to which of course we agreed. These boxes were of large size, of some dark red wood, bound and ornamented with quaint brass fittings. I cast longing eyes on some of the furniture of the houses we visited, for the chests were very old and quaint, while there were some curious cabinets, which looked as if they might be any age. In Soŭl they make a good deal of brass-mounted furniture of this description, which, with small low tables on which they place the dishes containing their food, satisfies the modest wants of a Korean, who sleeps on the floor and squats on his heels at other times.

Next day, being Sunday, we felt must be a day of rest, so

we got up late, and leisurely divided and packed our stores, for G.-A. and I had to part here. Owing to the harvest, which was now in full swing, we could not get more than six bearers, while we wanted nine or ten for the pair of us, as every scrap of food had to be carried on men's backs; wherefore I decided to return to the coast, as I had to go to Japan

HUNTER AND GUIDES, PO-CHÖN.

on my way back to Hong-Kong, whither I had pledged myself to the General to return as soon as possible.

Po-chön is a little bit of a place of twelve houses, partly on an island formed by the debris brought down by the river, which here runs west and falls into the Yalu at Ka-rim. The tops of the hills about are all on the same level, 4000 feet above the sea, and ages ago the "White Mountain" must have poured forth a tremendous flood of lava in a south and south-west direction; the rivers have gradually worked out in this deposit valleys to the depth of about 1000 feet, and I saw hardly any boulders or stones except of lava, tuff, or pumice.

After luncheon we ascended by a steep path the hill to the north of the village; near the top was a long deer-fence, about four feet high, in which at intervals were openings, each having a noose carefully set to catch the animals attracted to the enclosure by a patch of beans therein. Having outstripped G.-A., I came upon a fallow hind, which got up about five yards from me, but it only went ten yards and then stopped to gaze at me, going on feeding as I remained still, though evidently very suspicious of me. As I had no gun, after watching the animal for ten minutes, I went on across the flat top of the hill, about 500 yards broad, and from the northern edge we could see the "White Mountain." Where we stood was as nearly as possible 4000 feet above the sea, and a careful observation with a clinometer showed that all the ridges to the north, west, and south-west were about on the same level; and assuming the distance to the "White Mountain" to be thirty-three miles, as we made it out to be, the height of the mountain came to about 8600 feet (G.-A. subsequently with an aneroid made it about 8900 feet).

DISTANT VIEW OF PAIK-TU-SAN OR WHITE MOUNTAIN.

Its jagged peaks, gleaming white for the most part, though here and there streaked with black, towered far above anything in view from north-west to north-east. Below the peaks we could see a huge black lava cliff seamed with watercourses, which appeared to fall vertically into a black chasm beneath; between us and the "Paik-tu-san" was apparently a plain, covered with small larches, but we knew there must be numerous valleys in it, worn by the many feeders of the Yalu. The white appearance of the mountain, as we could see through a telescope, did not arise from snow, but was caused by pumice-stone and loose ashes. A thousand feet below us was the valley of the Yalu, or Amnok, as the Koreans name it, winding amidst the lava hills; here and there on the Manchurian side was a Chinaman's house in a clearing of the forest, surrounded by a high fence and piles of lumber, the cutting of which for floating down the river forms one means of livelihood, while smuggling and hunting help to support life. There is a good deal of trade across the northern border into Chinese and Russian Manchuria in the way of smuggled gold, but it is impossible to estimate its amount.

We returned to Po-chön with the intelligence that there was no snow on the "White Mountain," but were not believed, as it is a fixed conviction, embedded in the mind of every Korean, and sanctified by the tradition of ages, that the mountain is always covered with snow. The interpreter and Yeung were evidently in a desperate fright at going to the mountain, accounting for it by saying there was no joss-house on the top, and that although once upon a time a Korean did get to the top, yet the Spirit was so offended at his presumption, that he caused his neck (other accounts say his leg) to grow a yard longer! Yeung gave me a farewell letter to his wife to take down-country, thinking his last days were come, and his bones would be left on the "White Mountain." This letter I sent on to Mr. Stripling at Soŭl from Won-san, but I never heard if Mrs. Yeung received it.

A close cross-examination of the villagers produced nothing but a denial of any tigers being found near here, though Mr. Campbell in 1889 was told by a Chinese hunter just across the Yalu that there were a great many; the people owned to bears, deer, and pheasants, but of tigers and leopards they denied having any knowledge, though they admitted their existence in the forests nearer to the Paik-tu-san; and in this they were correct, for G.-A. found numerous fresh tracks of tigers on his way to and from the "White Mountain."

In questioning the natives, we found that Yeung, a Soŭl-bred man, had some difficulty in making himself understood here, where the dialect differed very much from that in use in the south, even to our uneducated ears. The word used for tiger hitherto had been "ho-rangi;" here this was not understood, as the word employed was "poom." The natives showed a greater acquaintance with Chinese, and the cook was able to talk a Chino-Korean mixture to them. Philologists tell us that the Korean alphabet is the most rational and simplest in the world, and it is devoid of the complex characters of the Chinese; but on account of its very simplicity it is only used by coolies and women; every educated and official person employs Chinese characters by which to express his ideas, so it is not surprising that many of the "mapus" could not read those characters written on the li-posts. A somewhat similar state of things exists in Japan, where the native daily papers are printed with the Chinese and Japanese characters in parallel columns, so that their contents may be read by low as well as high.

On Monday, October 5th, G.-A. started for the "White Mountain." Although his supply of food was most modest, and he had reduced his other impedimenta as much as possible, we found that, with a fortnight's provision of millet for Yeung, the interpreter, and six bearers, the weight of the loads caused much grumbling, notwithstanding that each man had only about 75 lbs. to carry. However, he got away by 9.30 A.M., and I accompanied him down the river to Ka-rim, a group of five huts, where the stream joined the Yalu. At the entrance to the village were a couple of new and remarkably hideous li-posts, and an official gateway something like a Japanese "torii," marking the boundary between the Kap-san and Sam-su districts.

As these were by far the ugliest presentments of the human countenance we had yet seen, we photographed one of them; the inscription showed it to be the 1330th li from Soŭl, which, viâ Puk-chong and Ham-heung, is fairly correct, though by the way we had come it was the 1617th. This photograph, like nearly all we took, turned out a failure. At Ka-rim we were kept waiting three-quarters of an hour, while G.-A.'s bearers bought, with much difficulty and at great expense, some little packets of rice, which they had been unable to procure at Po-chŏn. This rice was to be boiled on the "White Mountain" to propitiate the evil spirits who would come, and, after smelling the savoury odour of the mess, leave the adventurous party to eat their rice in peace. Whether our cook, whom I was taking down-country with me, could not get a sufficient price for it, or whether it was pure "cussedness" in not owning up to its possession, I do not know, but all the time he had some rice which he had brought from Won-san; for that very evening he gave me some excellent curried chicken and rice for dinner. On getting under way again, we crossed the Yalu in a dug-out, and found ourselves in Chinese Manchuria. Here G.-A. and I parted, much to my regret, as I had attained neither object of my journey—a visit to the White Mountain or tiger-shooting—but we had wasted so much time in one way and another that we had little hope of G.-A. getting to the mountain, as he was six days later than Mr.

Campbell, who had been stopped by snow in his ascent in 1889, and by the feigned sickness of his guide.

Crossing back into Korea with the Kap-san soldier, I climbed up the face of the mountain we had been on the day before, hoping to get a shot at deer, of which the tracks were plentiful. It was a hot and stiff climb over lava boulders and fallen trees, and once when clinging to the face of the cliff with one hand on the dead leaves, a brown adder glided out from beneath it; unluckily the soldier was carrying my gun, so the poisonous reptile escaped. Of course I saw no game on the top, but had a very fine view of the Paik-tu-san. Athough there had been five or six degrees of frost the previous night, there was no snow on the mountain, which so far augured well for the success of G.-A.'s expedition, though much might happen in the six days his journey thither was expected to occupy. I spent the afternoon in packing the stores, which the head-man had agreed to look after for G.-A., and in getting ready for an early start the next day, as I wanted to get back to Won-san as quickly as possible.

CHAPTER VIII.

THE ASCENT OF THE "WHITE MOUNTAIN."

THE little farm-house in which we stopped at Po-chŏn was most picturesquely placed on the north side of the stream; it was a quiet spot, not to say retired, and the inhabitants must lead very quiet lives. Their only little excitement during the year is a visit from a man-eating tiger, or when the droves of cattle accompanied by their drivers periodically pass through on their way to China or Wladivostock; on these latter occasions, I understand, the place is *en fête*, and as much wine is drunk as whisky is at an Irish wake.

In making preparations for the ascent of the "Paik-tu-san" or "White Mountain," I found that no longer could the faithful but ugly pony be used for transport work; the coolie took his place, and I had to walk, a slower but decidedly safer means of progression. Alas! only six coolies could be found, owing to the harvest having to be gathered in, and this number being far too few for us both, very much against my wish, my travelling companion, Cavendish, decided not to accompany me. I also learnt that there were two ways to the mountain, and that it was 200 miles high; the route on the left bank of the Amnok or Yalu was that traversed by Mr. Campbell in his attempt on the mountain in 1889; accordingly I decided to take the one on the right bank.

When we started from Po-chön on October 5th, my party

THE AMNOK OR YALU, NEAR THE "WHITE MOUNTAIN."

formed a motley crew, the coolies dressed in deer-skin breeches and coats, with conical felt hats with broad brims, my Korean interpreter (Yeung) in a long flowing coat, which had at one time been white, and the ordinary horse-hair Korean hat— he never could be induced to put on the more useful country-garb, he was far too great a town-swell for that! I myself was badly off for boots, one heel having given way, which necessitated my wearing the native footgear, wadded socks and straw sandals, after a short time.

Near Ka-rim, where the rice was bought, we crossed the Amnok in a cranky little dug-out. The river ran south-west amidst high hills clad to their summits with larches, and here and there a poplar; though now shallow, and about fifty yards broad, the current was swift, and when the snows melt, they must swell the river into a raging torrent, judging from the height of the banks, which are undermined and eaten away in many places. On the Manchurian bank I parted from Cavendish, after a series of photographs had been taken, not one of which turned out satisfactorily.

After saying good-bye, I and my party made our way down the river-bank till we came to a small log-hut inhabited by Chinamen, who were fairly civil, though they jeered at us, to help us on our way perhaps! Though there are many Chinese settlers on the southern slopes of the Chang-pai mountains, of which the Paik-tu-san is the principal, one does not meet with them again until this chain has been crossed, for most of the trapping and hunting in the mountains is done by Koreans, who cross the border into Manchuria in the early autumn or late summer, remaining there till compelled about November to return on account of the snow.

THE ASCENT OF THE "WHITE MOUNTAIN"   161

These Chinese are from the province of Shan-tung, and speak with that peculiar brogue, akin somewhat to the Irish, for which they are noted; they are a slovenly, dirty, cut-throat-looking lot of blackguards, and how they come to be so far from their own province I do not know. Some say they are discharged soldiers, and others that they are bad characters banished to the basin of the Amnok instead of to that of the Amoor.

They occupy themselves in felling the magnificent trees which abound on both banks, Korean and Chinese, of the Amnok, although they have no right to do so on the Korean side. Notwithstanding these trees being property appertaining to the Korean king, the authorities of that country are very loath to enforce any powers they may have against these plunderers, for fear of giving offence to their suzerain lord, the Emperor of China. Hence, far below Po-chön, in Korea itself, one finds Chinamen felling trees, which they have no right to touch, and this leads to much bad feeling, and not unfrequently to bloodshed. The trees thus felled, whether on the right bank or the wrong, are made into rafts and floated down to the mouth of the river, whence they find their way to various parts of China.

A few miles beyond this Chinese hut our path suddenly turned due north up the slope of the hill, and we found ourselves in the forest which extends all the way to the White Mountain and for miles beyond it. The moment we

L

got under the shade of the trees we found the cold intense; sombre and gloomy too it was, and half-a-dozen yards on each side of our path was the limit of our vision.

A mile or so within this forest, I encountered something in the way of game. I was carrying my gun at safety, when suddenly I flushed a couple of birds, and of course forgot to put the bolt forward. However, it did not matter, for, to my intense astonishment, they only flew a few yards and then perched on a tree. I am almost ashamed to say I shot them both, one waiting till the other had been disposed of. I afterwards ascertained that they were hazel-grouse (*Tetrao Omisia*). The coolies said they were good to eat, and I tried one that evening, but it was a decided failure, as it was tougher than the toughest beefsteak to be found in China. By keeping these birds a few days I always found them excellent eating; it may have been hunger, but certainly they seemed to me better than anything I had ever eaten in the way of game.

It was very difficult to make out the lie of the country on either side of the route on account of the thickness of the undergrowth, but evidently we were making our way up a spur lying between two tributaries of the Amnok, for from time to time we could hear the rush of water down below us on one side or the other. All day we continued ascending very gradually till we arrived at about 4100 feet above the sea, when we camped, or I should say bivouacked. There were no streams to be met with, so we had to content ourselves with burying a tin can in the moss and letting the water (for the ground was very boggy) overflow the edges. Trees were soon felled, and a large fire fifteen yards in length made up: the cold being intense, we much wanted a blaze. For food I had nothing but Liebig and brandy, except for weevilly biscuits and what game I shot. I was kind enough to offer the biscuits to my Koreans, but they politely refused to have anything to do with them; as I could not eat them myself, I threw them away, and had to fall back on boiled millet (the only food carried by the coolies). On this stuff I subsisted for seventeen days, an experience I do not want to again go through.

Before, however, we could sit down to our magnificent repast, the spirit whose domains we were invading had to be propitiated; for this purpose the rice had been brought. A miserable little pinch was cooked, spread out on the trunk of a fallen tree, and allowed to remain there for a quarter of an hour or so, until half cold; my men in the meantime (though professed Buddhists) standing in front, muttering, shaking their hands in Chinese fashion, and now and then expectorating. Their incantations finished, the rice was brought back to the fireside and solemnly eaten. They explained to me that the Spirit being such, could not eat rice, and only required the smell, so there could be no harm in their consuming this tiny luxury.

We soon lay down to sleep round the fire, and I then discovered that my two foolish interpreters had brought no covering with them, because somebody had told them it was dangerous to do so, for during the night they might roll over too close to the fire, and their blankets might catch fire. I had a blanket and two waterproof sheets, so felt constrained to give them each one of the latter ; very sorry I was too, for it first rained during the night, then froze, and when I tried to get up in the morning, it was just as if I was in a strait-waistcoat, and the blanket actually tore before I could unroll it.

That night, too, animals of some sort, which we could not make out, attracted no doubt by the light of the fire, kept up a continual howling and barking. I fancy they must have been jackals or something of that kind. Next day I tried to find their tracks, but failed to do so, for no footprint remained on the mossy ground covered with pine-needles.

Travelling day after day in much the same fashion—the view limited to that straight ahead or behind, for there was nothing but thick undergrowth on each side to be seen—became, to say the least, monotonous ; moreover, the going shortly became very bad. I really believe there are more fallen trees in that abominable forest than standing ones; every ten paces we met one of these obstacles lying in the path, which had to be negotiated somehow without going round it. After a time, the trees being so big, I found it better to scramble underneath them than to eternally vault or climb over. On my return journey through this part, I had the satisfaction of seeing the whole forest in a blaze; both the trees standing and those fallen were burning, and I had no longer to scramble over these obstacles, but simply to pick my way amongst those reduced to ashes, though I must say I burnt my Korean shoes and socks occasionally. The natives, when I returned to Korea, had the impertinence to say that my party was responsible for this fire, by not having on one occasion extinguished our camp-fire before starting in the morning. This story was spread by some casual trapper who happened to pass through Po-chön, and it was totally untrue, for our fires did not want much extinguishing, as a rule, and when they did, I always saw to it myself. There is a very heavy fine, if not some worse punishment, for those caught firing the forest. Justice is administered by the Guild mentioned by Mr. James (in his "Long White Mountain"), which looks after the interests of trappers in the Chang-pai mountains, as these fires are most destructive to the sable and beaver-trapping industry, which is very extensive in this part of the world. Whether the Koreans, who do most of the trapping, are in any way subject to this Guild I do not know, but I should fancy not.

After nine days' marching I at last found myself on the top of a spur which was devoid of trees. It was certainly *most* exhilarating. The sun was shining brightly, and not a cloud in the sky, though the wind was cold and piercing, and above all, the Paik-tu-san was in sight.

I was rather disappointed with it, for it looked so long, and without any corresponding height to carry off its length. It appeared so close that I fancied we might reach it by the next day at least; but I was very grievously mistaken, for now our troubles began. Hitherto we had been following a path used by cattle-drovers in taking their beasts to market in Manchuria from the Korean side, and we had progressed in the forest so far along this route that we were now actually abreast of the mountain on its west side; but before we could reach it we had to cross three ranges and three valleys—no mean undertaking without a path of any kind. My coolies were most unwilling to tread the sacred ground of Paik-tu-san, as it is considered to be unlucky, not to say dangerous. The natives firmly believe that dire punishment befalls those who intrude on the seclusion of the resident Spirit; even my highly educated interpreter (Yeung) was not above this foolish superstition. The coolies lost their way, or at least said they had, and begged me to return. "What more is wanted?" said they; "you have seen the mountain, and surely that is enough; you cannot possibly want to get to the very top."

Things very nearly came to a dead-lock, as they continued to press me to return, and dinned it into my ears that they had lost their way. However, one could not admit that the way was lost when our goal was absolutely in sight, and at no very great distance in a straight line.

After a time one of the men vouchsafed the remark that he knew of a sable-trapper in the vicinity, who might put us on our way. Accordingly he was sent in search of him, and, after about three hours, he and his friend the trapper made their appearance. I must say I was very much relieved, for certainly this man must be able to direct us.

We now made straight for the mountain, first, of course, descending to a valley where the trapper lived. The little valley he took us to was surrounded by hills, nearly 2000 feet above the hut, and formed a triangle. It reminded me somewhat of the description of the Hollance in "Robbery under Arms," it being quite flat, about ten acres in extent, and intersected by streams. There was, however, an absence of animal life which was most depressing. Perhaps the only living things to be found, after search, were woodpeckers, beavers, and sables, with a few pig and a bear or two, and now and then in the winter a tiger or a leopard.

Night was fast falling when we arrived at the trapper's little hut, but before anything could be done, the rice trick, with the same solemnity as before, had to be performed, for we were now under the special sway of the divinity of the Paik-tu-san. To further propitiate him, I was asked as a special favour, in a hardly audible whisper, to discharge a shot in the air. I need hardly say I was rather annoyed with the day's proceedings, and above all at this ridiculous proposition from a number of grown men. It was the case of the importunate widow, however, repeated for the millionth

KOREAN BEARERS.

time; so I discharged, not one, but both barrels in the air, after which we had our millet and went to bed.

The following day our route lay along the edge of a stream, of which the banks were fully 200 feet high. There was now no chance of our missing the way, as we took the trapper with us, leaving behind my oldest coolie in the solitary little hut to look after the traps in the owner's absence. All the coolies were fine stalwart fellows, but the hard work and bad food had told on them much. I therefore thought it advisable to leave behind the one most exhausted, so that he would be ready for work on my return journey. Poor old fellow! one night after arriving in camp, he was too exhausted to eat his millet, so I persuaded him to have a glass of brandy. Instead of drinking off, as most people (Europeans at least) would have done, he handed the mug round to all his fellow-coolies, each taking a sip, which left not very much for him. However, little as it was, it did him good, I was glad to see. His fellows were very good to him, carrying in turn his load in addition to their own, whenever he got fatigued; he also was never expected to cut down the dead trees for firewood; his business was to wash our millet and make the fire. I do not think I ever met better-natured men or more hard-working.

It was not always possible to see the stream we were following, but now and then, where the banks did not overhang, one could catch a glimpse of a roaring torrent, leaping over and circling round enormous boulders, which formed its bed, and carrying along on its current quantities of timber. My trapper told me this stream was a tributary of the Amnok; but this it could hardly be, as we were now on the northern slopes of the Chang-pai mountains, which in this part drain into the Sungari, to the north.

Landslips into the stream must be of daily occurrence, for many fractures in the soft volcanic soil looked quite fresh. Moreover, on more than one occasion I saw a tree or two with a quantity of earth gracefully glide down the bank and disappear in the water beneath. Numbers of trees which had only slipped a short way were to be seen standing on these precipitous banks in drunken-looking attitudes, and it was a marvel how they managed to stick there. The trees at this elevation, 6600 feet, were stunted in their growth, but towards evening we encamped at 400 feet lower. The weather had become intensely cold; it froze hard day and night, and a piercing wind was always blowing from the north-west; so much so, that none of us slept at night as we lay huddled round the fire, first warming one side and then the other.

Another day's travelling, and we found ourselves actually on the mountain we had come so far to ascend. During the day we met an ancient Korean trapper, with a flowing white beard and long grey hair. He presented a most uncouth appearance as he approached us with a hearty laugh, which made one start, so incongruous did it appear amidst these silent mountains, where no sound but the soughing of the wind through the tree-tops or the trickling of water far down below was to be heard. This old man kept my retainers all laughing for some time at his anecdotes, and eventually my aristocratic friend, Yeung, from the capital, began to chaff him as being a countryman. However, he got the worst of it; for, quite in a friendly way of course, the old trapper set upon him with his stick and trounced him right royally, both laughing all the while, but I could see that Yeung did not like it at all. I was delighted, for I had long wished something of the sort would happen, as all Koreans from Soŭl are most bumptious

CHINESE HUNTER'S LODGE.

and overbearing in their dealings with their less fortunate countrymen.

A constant ascent all day brought us at nightfall to a plateau 6200 feet above the sea, along which we walked for some miles through pleasant groves and very high grass, of which the greater part was now, being late autumn, lying on the ground. About 6 P.M. the solitary hut which belongs to a

Chinese settler came in sight, and very glad we were, for we were all much fatigued. We expected to be able to get some food of some sort here on payment, but were disappointed at finding nothing but potatoes; even these were a great luxury, and I made an excellent dinner with their aid.

It turned out that there was a second Chinaman belonging to the establishment, for when I lay down on the "kang" to sleep, we were told by the owner we must leave a place for his friend. We were very tightly packed, so much so that I did not sleep a wink, for Yeung, who had fought for the honour of sleeping next me, kept turning in his sleep, ousting me from my place and jamming me against the wall. He snored, too, abominably, though I woke him up a dozen times at least, warning him that I would throw him off the "kang" if he continued doing so; but all in vain.

Although we were now on the plateau whence the mountain springs, no information could be gathered from our Chinese hosts as to how we should make the ascent, for they were much too superstitious ever to have attempted it themselves, and, in fact, they confessed as much. Messrs. James, Fulford, and Younghusband made the ascent from this hut, having reached it from the north, but I could get no information as to the exact route they had followed to the summit. Therefore, accompanied by Yeung and the trapper, I decided to make straight for what looked like the highest peak. The remainder of the party refused to have anything to do with the ascent, as they did not wish to bring down the wrath of the Paik-tu-san spirit on their stupid heads. I did not mind much, as I knew I must be back long before dark. I had flattered myself that all of them would have been willing to make the ascent, for in the middle of the previous night all had gone off to a small building of logs close by, where they carried out the usual rites of mumbling, hand-shaking, rice-offering, and expectoration. The ceremony was more impressive than any I had experienced before, and tended to wakefulness on my part. This impressiveness I thought would clear the atmosphere and embolden them to beard the Spirit of the Mountain without danger; but not so, and I had to proceed with only two men.

The first half of the ascent was through grass now laid by the winds and rain, then stunted larch and birch trees, with here and there azalea bushes; these, when in bloom in summer, must make a pretty show. Till within about a thousand feet of the summit the climb was easy, the incline not being very steep, but the latter part, however, was most toilsome, as our feet sank deep at every step in the powdered pumice, which here covers everything.

After a climb of 2700 feet from the hut, the summit of the mountain, if one may call it so, was reached. I thus made the height to be 8900 feet above sea-level. As a matter of fact, the Paik-tu-san being an extinct volcano, has no summit; that part, if it ever existed, having been blown out long ago. The crater thus made is now full of water, and forms a large lake some dozen miles in circumference and nearly circular in shape. Arrived between two of the twenty or more peaks which stud the circumference, one unexpectedly finds oneself in presence

THE LAKE ON THE "WHITE MOUNTAIN."

of this lake; so suddenly does it come into view, that one is quite startled.

It was a striking scene; the absolute stillness and intense blueness of the lake contrasted strongly with the hurricane raging about me and the grey and white slopes beneath me. The stillness of the surface was accounted for by the protection afforded by the peaks, for the lake lay 250 or 300 feet below the rim of the crater. Not a living thing of any description was to be seen, and no marks of animals such as were to be found half way down. Tracks were there innumerable of pigs and deer, the ground everywhere around being rooted up by the former, which, I am informed, are found in great numbers on the lower slopes.

The view from the top is magnificent, for one towers far above the surrounding country for many miles; except towards Kirin, the eye rests on nothing but forest, with here and there a bare patch. Towards Kirin we fancied we could see the smoke of some village or town rising from behind an undulation in the plain, which stretches in that direction for miles and miles.

I wish I had been able to get some of the lake-water for analysis, to ascertain if there was any chemical cause for its intense blueness; but it was impossible, the sides being almost everywhere sheer, and the foot-hold in the crumbling pumice most precarious.

Having taken a number of photographs, to make sure of some result this time, I retraced my footsteps to the hut, where I arrived late in the afternoon.

Whilst intently observing the opposite shore of the lake with my telescope, I suddenly heard, as I thought, a gurgle behind me, and turning round, found Yeung holding to his lips my flask of precious brandy, which I had given him to carry. I thought it an excellent opportunity to give him that chastisement which he so richly deserved for all his lies, for having quarrelled with all my coolies, and on our way up to Po-chön driven away without our knowledge, and the poor man's *douceur*, a Yamen runner or "soldier" kindly lent to us by the Prefect of Won-san. I accordingly did so, the trapper looking on grinning. Yeung served me much better after this, though, like all interpreters in China and Korea, he could not help lying.

They resent being asked questions very much, and will give any reply, if they think one will believe it, so that they need not bother themselves to ask for the required information. On one occasion I asked him the name of a mountain close to our path, and he replied at once with a name out of his own head. I asked him how he happened to know, never having been in the locality before: his only reply was, "Why do foreigners always ask the name of this place and that mountain? What good can it do? There is the place, and there is the mountain: what more do they want?" It was the same with regard to the two hideous li-posts outside Kirin; they stood ten feet in height; the heads were roughly but ludicrously carved, and had real hair, eyebrows, and moustache stuck on with gum; the noses were painted red, and the eyes had a bloodshot appearance. They were quite new, and had lately been consecrated with "wine," for the splashes were still to be seen on the yellow wood. Yeung told me they were "joss-pidgin," *i.e.*, sacred, and the inscription showed this was the 1330th li from Soŭl, but he could not translate more of it than that. Why they should have been put there, I could not understand, unless to serve as an imaginary gateway from one district to another. In passing from one province to another, one always finds a gateway, generally consisting of two poles and a crossbar, like a "torii," but there is no gate, and as often as not the road passes some yards off on one side or the other. However, Yeung was equal to the occasion, and his ready lie was, that whenever an official of high rank changed his name, he put up one of these gateways as an offering to the particular spirit of that region. This I know to be an absolute falsehood. My Chinese interpreter was just the same, I am sure, but as he could not talk English nor I Chinese, I cannot say I actually convicted him of lying.

To resume my story, just after reaching the hut, the sky became overcast, and in a short time down came the snow. It was fortunate that it had held off so long, for had it come on twenty-four hours sooner, I could not have made the ascent. As it was, it had all along been touch and go, for we started on our expedition much too late in the year, but this we did not know until we arrived in Korea; it was the snow which stopped Mr. Campbell in 1889, and he was six days earlier than I was.

It had been my intention, after having visited the "White

Mountain," to push on to Kirin, thence by Mouk-den to Newchwang, where I could take the steamer; but this idea I had to abandon at Po-chön, where I had to leave my stores, clothing, money, &c., for I heard it was impossible to get transport either in the form of coolies or mules, and my Korean followers refused to go farther into Manchuria than the Paik-tu-san. Could I have gone this way, it would have saved an immense amount of trouble and discomfort, for I should not have had to re-cross the Chang-pai mountains.

In order to test the accuracy of this information, I visited the nearest Chinese village, about seven miles off, where I was again informed nothing could be got in the way of transport unless I was content to wait till it could be sent for from Kirin. Moreover, that, as China was at war with some foreign country (the name of which I could not discover), whose troops had invaded Manchuria, it would be just as well to give Kirin and the neighbourhood a wide berth. It must be remembered I had not seen a newspaper for two months. Accordingly I retraced my steps, and proceeded south to Po-chön over much the same country as I had before traversed. In all, I was seventeen days away from that village, and very pleased was I to get back there, for I was able at length to get some suitable food; not much, perhaps, for everything I had was tinned, and nothing whatever could be bought. Being much weakened by bad food for so long,

I determined to remain at Po-chŏn for a few days to recruit a little, and until ponies could be procured from Un-chong, the nearest posting establishment. What an abomination a tinned sausage is, or even tinned beef, unless one has gone without meat of any sort for a fortnight.

I amused myself here by fishing for trout with a native angler. His rod was most primitive, simply a fairly straight stick with about ten feet of gut fastened to the end, and an artificial fly was attached. I examined this curiosity intently, whereupon the owner proceeded to produce a naked hook from some fold of his garments, plucked out some hair from his deer-skin coat, placed it round the hook, tied it with some fine gut, and the fly was made. The hook I learnt, through my interpreter Yeung, the fisherman made himself. This was evidently untrue, for it was finished and japanned, and he probably got them through Wladıvostock or Won-san. After a couple of hours' fishing we had killed over forty small trout between us, averaging under half-a-pound each, but the Korean landed the major portion. I had been told that foreign flies were no good in Korea, and they certainly do not seem to be so effective as the native monstrosities. The native fly I tried, but could do nothing with it, and had to give it up.

After a few days' rest, and my ponies having arrived, I started for Kap-san. My coolies came to see me off, bringing eggs and honey as presents. I really hardly knew them, they looked so fresh and clean in their quaint Korean hats and long-flowing, cotton-quilted white coats; moreover, they had washed, and were no longer brown, but white.

The Northern Koreans are not the same race, I am certain, as the Southern, for they are not the same idle, good-for-nothing set, but, on the contrary, are as hard-working and industrious as possible. Besides this, from Kap-san to the northern border the natives have long features, with aquiline noses, and the almond-shaped eye and high cheek-bone so noticeable in Korea farther south, are almost entirely absent; as might be expected, the dialect differs also in a marked degree.

I took it very easy on my journey to the coast, only doing half marches, which annoyed Yeung very much, as he was in great haste to get back to Soül, to be present at his sister's wedding; at least, so he said. The truth was, I found out afterwards, that having used our names, without our sanction, to impress transport for himself on the journey up, he feared the authorities at Won-san would be on the look-out for him, and if they caught him, they would doubtless "paddle" him, a process very repugnant to the feelings of a self-respecting Korean. It consists in laying the culprit on his face and administering chastisement with a very long and broad flat stick to the place where his nether garment should be, but is not on these occasions.

On reaching Neun-gwi, I took the road to Puk-chöng, instead of that by which we had come. As we got nearer the coast, it became less and less cold, though we still had to sleep upon the "kang" every night or get frozen. The Korean "kang" is indeed a vast improvement on the Chinese one, for the fire being outside or in another room, the blinding smoke in one's bedroom is avoided.

The shooting to be got between Puk-chong and Won-san was extraordinary; swans, geese, and ducks in countless numbers. All day, as we passed along, we saw them in the recently cut paddy-fields, picking up the grains of rice which had fallen out of the ears. They were quite easy to approach, no device of any kind being required; even when one did fire a shot, the birds simply flew a short distance, and others perhaps took their places. Pheasants and quail there were, too, in great abundance, but the former were not so confiding as the ducks by any means, and required a good deal of stalking; besides, without a dog it was extremely difficult to flush them.

Thus, by easy stages I reached Won-san, where I intended to take the steamer for Chefoo and Tientsin; but as the weather at sea was very stormy, I did not do so, but proceeded overland to Soül, where I arrived on November 19.

H. E. GOOLD-ADAMS.

HONG-KONG, 1893.

CHAPTER IX.

PO-CHÖN TO WON-SAN.

ON October 6th, leaving seventeen packages for G.-A., I started at 8.40 A.M. with four animals (three post-ponies and, for my riding, the grey mare which G.-A. had ridden from Won-san). Through the cook the mare's attendant volunteered to come down to Won-san with me for what I paid the post-ponies, *i.e.*, 50 cash per stage or 100 cash per diem. However, when I reached Won-san, he claimed to be paid at the original rate of 11 cash per li, or about ten times higher. Of course he laid the blame of the misunderstanding on the cook; but as he was a fairly good swindler himself, I eventually compounded with him for 2860 cash, or 6000 less than he asked. The cook had started from Won-san with nothing but an advance of two dollars, and professed to keep an accurate account of what he paid for our food, and that of the servants, &c. Yet he had enough cash to take me back there, disbursing some 6500 cash for me! When I reached Won-san, he told me he wanted to go back to Soŭl, so I paid him his fare by steamer to the capital; but the heathen Chinee once more proved his superiority to the simple Western, and, waiting for G.-A.'s return, he accompanied him as cook overland to Soŭl! In leaving Po-chön he had started ahead of me, but when I got to the top of the ridge from the river, he was not to be seen, but, as I subsequently found out, had gone to the houses, where he had encountered the Chinamen two nights before, while I had gone round outside the enclosure and so missed him. Consequently, when I got down to the hut where we caught up the baggage-ponies on the evening of the 5th, I had to wait an hour for him.

Some of the pines in this forest were magnificent in size, and all were as straight as masts and of fair height, but the torch-carrying had caused many small fires to arise, and the blackened trunks looked very melancholy. There was not, however, the same wholesale destruction which we had encountered farther south. In places the ground was covered with a giant-kind of maidenhair fern about two feet in height.

From the top of the ridge above the river I obtained, through the vista made by the road, a splendid view of the White Mountain. From the hill above Po-chön the full effect of the view of the mountain was dwarfed by the intervening thirty miles of country being practically on the same level as my eye. But from this point, 700 feet higher, these thirty miles were spread out beneath my view, and I could better appreciate how strikingly this mountain stands out above its surroundings. As far as the eye could reach on this brilliant sunny day, from north-west to north-east (the forest limiting my angle of vision to this quadrant), this extinct volcano towered in solitary grandeur 4700 feet above everything else, and the rest of the country appeared an unbroken pine-clad plain, though I knew that the many streams flowing north, south, and east to form the Sungari, Yalu, and Tumen rivers had worn deep valleys through the vast crust of volcanic matter which in remote time had been spread over the land by this remarkable mountain. I could well understand how its mysterious isolation had given birth to the many legends and myths concerning it current amongst the nature-worshipping races who at different times have peopled its vicinity. When I say the Paik-tu-san towered 4700 feet above everything else, I must explain that in my opinion the mountain ridges, from 5000 to 6000 feet high, which stand at its feet, are the remains of a yet larger and more ancient volcano, in the midst of which, after a lengthened period of quiescence, the present Paik-tu-san was elevated in a final effort of the subterranean forces.

Here too, in a little glade, were three small joss-houses, and, as the cook gave me to understand, annually on the fourth day of the eighth moon, sacrifices are made by the representatives of the King of Korea at this point in view of the Paik-tu-san to the Spirit of the Mountain, to whose influence, according to Korean legend, the origin of the race is to be ascribed.

The soldier tried to take me round by the same way as we had come from Un-chong, but I detected him in time, and reached that place at 2.20 P.M. I put up at a dirty little inn, to avoid the delay caused by going to the head-man's house, leaving again at 4.40, and stopped for the night at 8 P.M. at Sun-yun-i, a small village 5 li from Tong-in, having had torches from An-kang-poi, a hamlet at the northern side of the An-kang pass.

I reached Kap-san at 11 A.M. the next day, and again put up at the official house. I found everything we had left behind quite safe, including the cash, but the extra baggage entailed two more post-ponies. After luncheon I had the ponies loaded and started them off, going then myself, with the cook as interpreter, to call on the Prefect. The curiosity of the inhabitants was still great, and they crowded round me examining every article of clothing I had on, but perfectly civil all the time. Having thanked the Prefect for his attentions and care of our property, I asked him to send the soldier back to Po-chön in ten days' time to meet G.-A., and if the latter had not returned from the Paik-tu-san by then, to send in search of him. This the Prefect kindly said he would do and sent another soldier with me. The interpreting was rather difficult, as the cook understood but little English, and could not talk much polite Korean. There are different phrases and inflections in the language (as in Japanese), according to whom one is addressing, a superior, an equal, or an inferior, and the cook could only speak the inferior or coolie language. We had often heard Yeung and the cook talking in pidgin-English, because the former could not be talked to as if he was the inferior.

The day being cold, with frequent showers, the cook fortified himself here with some samshu, which first made him drunk, and then upset him completely. He looked a miserable object all the afternoon, and at length turned into a house and lay down on his stomach on the "kang" to get warm. As he had been ill over part of my things, I did not pity him very much, and went on; but as he did not catch me up by the time I reached Ho-rin at 5.30 P.M., I stopped there for the night. Thoughts of my pleasant position should the cook be taken seriously ill or die, caused me to welcome him on his arrival in better condition at 9 P.M. with much relief!

On October 8th, starting at 6 A.M. with the thermometer at 31° and a strong and bitter north-west wind blowing, I had a very cold journey to Neun-gwi, where I changed ponies and felt thoroughly chilled, as I had to wait an hour while the animals were obtained. Leaving again at 9.40 A.M., I crossed the river by the permanent bridge, and took the main road to the coast and Puk-chöng. The going was no better than on any other road, and the ascent of a pass 4600 feet above sea-level was terribly difficult, a constant clamber over roots of fir-trees and boulders set in slippery black mud. I waited three-quarters of an hour at the top for the baggage-animals, and then descended to Chan-ka-cham, where I stopped two hours to change ponies. On starting again, the road followed a stream for 5 li in an easterly direction, and then turned sharp round a spur to the W.S.W. up another stream. By this time it was getting dark, and with some difficulty torches were procured, and by their aid we got over a wooded pass 5050 feet above sea-level. Very glad was I to stop for the night at half-past eight at Houng-so-wŏn, for it had been bitterly cold all day, and the miserable ponies kept falling down with their loads, although they had only come from Chan-ka-cham.

Finding five ponies were incapable of carrying my baggage without falling, I procured six here, and started at 7 A.M. next morning. The wind had fallen, luckily, and I felt less uneasy about G.-A.; it was a good thing for me too, for the thermometer was only 24° in the shade. The crisp frosty air invited one to walk, so invigorating was it. Houng-so-wŏn is situated on the edge of a plain plentifully bestrewn with blocks of lava and surrounded by forest-clad mountains, through gaps in which two streams escape to the E.N.E.

Descending to the southernmost of these streams at the end of the plain, we next got to the top of the Hu-chih-ryöng at 10.40 A.M., and stopped at a small village for fifteen minutes while the "mapus" got some food. Here a dog actually smelt my hand and allowed me to pat him without snapping or barking. This was the only one out of the hundreds of curs we met which condescended to speak in a friendly manner to the white man.

By a steep zigzag path I descended 1500 feet to the Nam-ta-che-ni river, flowing south-east, which 10 li farther on turned south through a narrow gorge, and I got to Chyei-in-koan at two o'clock. The line of demarcation between long low huts with birch-bark roofs, and those with curled tile or thatch ones was abruptly marked at this pass, which at the same time was the extreme boundary of the forest-clad mountains. The Paik-un-san chain, which I was leaving behind me, forming the backbone and watershed of Korea, seems to divide the inhabitants, their dwellings, and the vegetation into distinct varieties.

At Chyei-in-koan I could only get five very bad ponies led by little boys, and the loads kept continually slipping. The valley now widened somewhat into a stony waste from a quarter to half a mile in width. The river running under precipitous hills on its right bank, while on its left numerous short valleys contributed wide stony watercourses, most wearisome to cross. I noticed great quantities of dazzling white quartz rocks and boulders, and rapid denudation seemed to be going on, for everywhere the surface earth was slipping from the higher levels. At Sigori, whence a footpath goes to Phyöng-an, we got torches, and stumbled along a very bad road in the dark, till we reached Chang-heung at 7.30 P.M. The magistrate here is a second-class prefect, and my passports and card had to be sent to him before the post-superintendent could give me any ponies.

Getting nearer the coast I found the clothing of the peasantry changing from the coloured cottons of Chinese make, to which we had been accustomed farther north, to the ordinary white, and in the village shops a few foreign goods began to appear, such as Japanese matches, dyes, ribbons, &c. However, at Un-chong I was able to buy both Chinese and Japanese matches, excessively cheap at 5 cash or two-fifths of a penny per box, but I am still in doubt as to which make was the worst.

October 10*th*.—Chang-heung being only 600 feet above the sea, I found the air quite warm at starting this morning at 6.50 A.M. The ponies provided for me were worse than ever to look at, and two of them were simple frameworks partially covered with skin and hair. How they got along at all was a constant source of wonder to me, but they did it, and at a fair pace too—45 li in 3¾ hours!

190 KOREA AND THE SACRED WHITE MOUNTAIN

After passing two villages, Noyada and Chöngmoru, each standing in a sea of rice-fields, I arrived at Puk-chöng at 10.15 A.M. This place is the seat of a second-class prefecture, and is surrounded by a wall with earth backing, about 20 feet high, enclosing a square of about 800 yards to a side. The post-superintendent made objections to giving

PUK-CHÖNG, LOOKING SOUTH-WEST.

me ponies, so the cook, bearing my card and papers, went with him to the Prefect, and after waiting three hours I got my ponies. The inhabitants were decidedly rude, calling me "Cheenaman," and taking Macaulay's Essays, which I sat and read, for a Chinese book!

Leaving here at 1.30, 1 crossed the river, which reaches

the sea 10 li farther down, and struck into the low hills to the south-west, crossing numerous small streams running east to the sea. I was now on the high-road from Wladivostock to Won-san, and found it better going, but by no means level. About four o'clock we ascended a few hundred feet to a narrow saddle, Pa-mun Ryöng, between two hills, where there was just room for the road, and then descended to the horribly stony valley of the Bu-si-ka-chi river, about one mile wide, in which grew rice, tobacco, and beans, and arrived at Pyöng-po-ri at 7 P.M. The hills here were of the same desolate character as about Won-san, disintegrating red granite with a few fir trees dotted about.

We came in sight of the Sea of Japan next day at 9 A.M., and travelled along the shore for about two miles; a fringe of fir-trees and then a fringe of graves separating the road from the almost tideless ocean, for on the east coast of Korea the tidal change only amounts to eighteen inches. Ho-wön stands about two miles inland, and at the south end of the bay, which we had skirted, is Choll-nam, a small fishing village. The road now ran along cliffs, about 100 feet above the sea, to Houng-wön on the river Shika, at the edge of another plain, and I should imagine this had formerly been an inlet of the sea by the look of the hills surrounding it. Here I changed ponies, and was given another soldier in place of the man I had brought from Puk-chöng. The young fellow who had come with me from Kap-san to the coast was bitterly disappointed at not being allowed to go on to Won-san, and shed tears on parting with me at Puk-chöng. While at luncheon in the inn, the proprietor came to look at me, but kindly kept everybody else away. He asked for a taste of whisky and a cake, which I gave him, much to his satisfaction and that of a friend for whom he asked a similar favour.

On starting again from Houng-wön with fresh animals, a dilapidated little pony carrying my cartridge magazine and the cook's box, each weighing about 90 lbs., got frightened at the rattling of the kettle which was tied on to his pack, and bolted, crossing at a gallop a bridge which was much out of repair, but was stopped in about half a mile by some Koreans. Near here I passed another fenced-in graveyard, and apparently to-day was an anniversary day, for most of the population appeared to be in the graveyards worshipping their ancestors or re-burying them; but for fear of complications arising through want of a Korean interpreter, I avoided going near any of the functions I saw proceeding. A little farther on we came to the Government archery-ground, a patch of turf about 200 yards long by 20 wide, with a belt of fir-trees on each side, and a small official shed as a firing-point. Across the plain we went on towards a high range of hills, and after changing ponies again at Hamheung-cha'in,

we reached the foot of the pass (Hang-kal-ryöng) at 4.30 P.M. At a little hamlet here a halt took place, while my attendants endeavoured to get some men to carry up part of the baggage, as the ponies were so bad; but the villagers all refused, so we went on. I was rather mystified here by the cook telling me we had to cross "a big i-land," by which I thought he meant a piece of land entirely surrounded by water, but seeing no water about, it at length dawned on me he meant "a big highland!" High it was, about a thousand feet up and down, but a zigzag path with a gradient of 10° enabled us to surmount it without much difficulty, though it was a long pull up. On the way down my mare kicked me on the thigh as I was walking beside her, but fortunately did me no damage. The pass was thickly covered with oaks, sycamores, and Scotch firs, nearly all covered with virginia creeper in autumn colouring. At the foot of the pass we found the village of Tong-sa-mi, beside a river running through a remarkably stony gorge, and here, at 5.50 P.M., we stopped for the night, as the nearest place was 30 li farther on. This was not a posting-station, which accounted for our changing ponies at Hamheung-cha'in. In the evening a disturbance was caused by some of the "mapus" demanding beans for their ponies from the woman at whose house they were lodged. She protested she had none, so they abused and threatened her, whereupon she rushed up to the head-man, in whose house I was, to complain, and for half-an-hour I listened to torrents of Billingsgate, varied by floods of tears and sobs of rage. Eventually she was pacified, and the village settled down for the night.

Starting at 6.15 A.M. on the 12th, we followed the river down to Tong-sang-kuan, where I got some better ponies, led by some smart boys, and the road across the plain being level and good, we did the 30 li into Ham-heung in 2½ hours. The wide plain of the valley of the Kho-ta river, made up of fields of rice, beans, millet, &c., with watercourses banked up for irrigation purposes, stretched to the walls of the capital of the province, and was simply crowded with pink ibis, cranes, wild geese, and duck, but I was in too great a hurry to stop very long to shoot. We skirted the wall of the town for some distance, and off-saddled at noon at a large inn, crowded with Koreans, near the south gate.

On sending to the head pony-man for ponies, he said he could not give them without the consent of the Governor and Prefect, who were at some place 60 li off. As I had done 614 li in 6½ days, which was very fair going, I did not want to be delayed here, so I went off to see the Mandarin next in importance. I found him at home in a little ordinary Korean house, in the yard of which millet, rice, and strings of chillies were drying in the sun. "No. 3 Mandarin" was dressed in blue and scarlet silk robes, and wore a black military hat with a peacock's feather in it, and was very distant in his manner. I was offered a bale of Manchester shirting as a seat, and unfolded the object of my visit with some difficulty, as "No. 3" could not or would not understand what the cook said. However, he sent for the head pony-man, an insolent-looking man, and ordered him to give me six ponies at once. He also said he would send another soldier with me. Having thanked him, I went back to mine inn, and waited patiently for ponies. First the pony-man came to say he had to send 10 li for them, and could not get them before the next morning. This was not true, for while the cook was away six ponies were sent for me, but in his absence I could not get them loaded, or ascertain for certain they were mine. Next the Governor returned, and my papers had to be sent to him by hand of the cook. This occupied the time till 6.15 P.M., when the cook returned with a promise from the pony-man that I should have the ponies at 6 A.M. next morning. Being thus forced to stop here for the night, I got a small room used by the "mapus," which was filthily dirty, evil-smelling, and thickly populated with various insects. The big room of the inn was full of Koreans, whose habits were such as to prevent me eating or sleeping near them.

Whilst waiting in the inn to-day, I had plenty of opportunities of observing the nauseous smell of the food greedily devoured by the Koreans. Five or six little dishes, containing various preparations of meat or fish, chillies, beans, cabbage, rice, &c., were ranged on a little table a foot high, and gave forth a most evil odour. A Korean likes his viands very highly seasoned, and in eating takes a little of every dish into his mouth, that he may enjoy the pleasant mingling of the different flavours. My sleep was disturbed by dreaming of a Korean I had seen in the afternoon, whose nose had been entirely eaten away by disease, and his face was horrible to look at. I have mentioned before that in the more northern and wilder districts we did not notice so many traces of disease, but now, on one of the most frequented highways of the country, I began to find again women with diseased breasts, men showing traces of virulent syphilis, and also deformities of various kinds.

I breakfasted at 6½ A.M. next morning, but no ponies appeared, and in answer to several messages, I was always told they were just finishing their morning feed. At length, about eight, I went to the Governor's Yamen, but it was too early for me to see him, or for him to see my card; so I waited there half-an-hour, sending the cook back to the inn to see if the ponies had turned up. At the end of that time he returned with the welcome intelligence that six ponies were there; so leaving my card for the Governor with my thanks for the ponies, I hastened back, glad to escape from the curious and insolent crowd of Yamen loafers and hangers-on, whose jeers and insults I had endured for so long. Alas! on reaching the inn, there were no ponies! The explanation given was, that last night the Prefect had ordered six for me, while this morning the Governor said two were enough for me. Very soon after this, the card of the Governor of the Hamgyong province, whose name is Han-Chang-Sok, arrived, but still no ponies. Again visiting the Yamens of the Governor and the

HAM-HEUNG BRIDGE, LOOKING SOUTH-EAST.

Prefect, who were both too sick to see me (the usual form of refusing an interview), the latter refused to accept my card, after keeping me waiting for an hour; so I gave up attempting to get ponies from the officials, and going back to the inn, with a little bargaining, I hired five ponies to go to Wonsan, each at 8 cash per li. Quickly loading up, I started at noon, crossing the So-chön river by the trestle bridge, 470 yards long, accompanied by a soldier whom the Prefect had sent to conduct me. When I say I crossed by the bridge, I mean I got half-way across, but then found it was under repair, and in attempting to swing myself across the gap, I slipped off, and sat down in the shallow river, to the huge delight of the onlookers, who shouted with laughter. I did not laugh at all! The final result of my difficulties about ponies at Ham-heung, was that two days after my arrival at Won-san the Prefect of Tök-wön told me he had received 10,800 cash from the Prefect of Ham-heung to reimburse me for the hire of the ponies, as he regretted he had been unable to procure any ponies for me! I, of course, pretended to swallow the lies and sent back the money, but whether it ever reached the Prefect of Ham-heung I cannot say.

Ham-heung is partly built on the side of a spur running out into the plain, the Governor's residence and garden running up to the wall which crosses the ridge. The town is surrounded by a stone wall, 20 feet high and 6 or 8 feet thick, strengthened with an earthen banquette; but it is much out of repair and in many places has fallen down. The narrow and devious lanes, however, in many cases rejoiced in side-ditches to carry off rain-water, &c., and each house had a fence or wall round it. Outside the walls on the flat a suburb was growing up, and in the little shops the usual mixture of native and foreign merchandise was exposed for sale. I obtained some very good pears here, like green jargonel, at the ridiculously small cost of one cash each, and very excellent eating they were.

Journeying over the plain of rice-fields, and crossing several shallow sandy streams, I at 4 P.M. reached Chyöng-phyöng, where I was glad to get my luncheon after my early breakfast. I left this again at 6½ P.M., and, aided by a brilliant moon, got to Cho-wön at 10 P.M., myself and everything else soaked by the heavy dew. I reached Yeung-heung at 10 A.M. on the following day, having done 45 li in 3¼ hours, and, after ferrying over the river, halted for luncheon for three hours. Here I found the cook had carefully forgotten to put the cork in my one whisky-bottle, and as it had been carried mouth downwards in the provision-box, I had to fall back on tea. Having changed soldiers at Yeung-heung and Ko-wön, I arrived at 4.30 P.M. at So-rai-wön, where the "mapus" insisted on stopping to give their ponies a small feed of beans, their third meal this day. I walked on a good way, sat down on a pile of telegraph poles to wait for them, but at length walked back to meet them, which I did at eight o'clock, only half-a-mile from the village, and then they were going as slowly as possible with a torch, although the moonlight was as bright as possible. I hurried them on, but the result was I did not get to Mun-chön until 11 P.M., nor dine till 12.45 A.M.!

Between Yeung-heung and So-rai-wön I saw myriads of

wild geese, duck, teal, widgeon, &c., coming in from Port Lazareff to settle in the rice-fields for the night. The inhabitants were all abroad, with drums, tomtoms, and crackers, trying to frighten them away. I might have shot any number of them, only that I thought they would be so numerous at Won-san that it would be like carrying coals to Newcastle to bring in much more game.

On October 15th I once more found myself in Won-san. Notwithstanding that my room at Mun-chön was thickly populated with fleas, Norfolk Howards, &c., I slept soundly, and did not leave until eight o'clock. Deputing the cook to bring on the baggage, I hastened on with my "mapu" to Won-san, where I arrived at 11.40 A.M., having done the 260 li from Ham-heung in a little less than forty-eight hours, which was considered the best record known. But for the delay at Ham-heung, I should have done the distance from Po-chön, 874 li, in 8½ days, and the cook would have got the five dollars I had promised him if I got to Won-san in nine days. Very pleased was I to see some white faces again, unmistakably belonging to middies, and on inquiry I found that the British fleet under Sir Frederick Richards was lying in Port Lazareff. Brazier met me at the Custom-house, and told me I was to put up in Oiesen's house, he being expected back from Japan that evening. Once more I say how delicious was the first bath and the first drink of beer!

The night after I got to Won-san, Trollope the missionary turned up, having come from Soül by the Diamond Mountains in fourteen days. He had left his companion, Peek, who was footsore, with the baggage, and walked on. They lived in one of Knott's houses, and came up to Oiesen's to mess, until they left for Phyöng-an on the 21st. They told us some interesting yarns about the monasteries in Kang-wön province and their priests, who possess some very old MS. books, many of which are grossly indecent and obscenely illustrated. Trollope and Peek had been preceded in their journey by the two Germans I mentioned once before as shooting chickens, and everywhere, even in the most sacred spots, they found their names engraved in true tourist fashion on the rocks, which for more reasons than one was a very brazen proceeding. My steamer did not start for some days, and I enjoyed Oiesen's hospitality until October 23rd, leaving that evening for Fu-san and Yokohama, thus ending my holiday in Korea.

CHAPTER X.

ON SPORT IN KOREA.

OUR original object in going to Korea was to shoot tigers or leopards, for the tales we heard of their number, size, and ferocity, and of the beauty of their fur, made our mouths water; but the mysterious White Mountain lured us on to hasten to make its acquaintance, and partly on that account the shooting was somewhat of a failure.

Without doubt there is a great quantity of game in Korea, but there is only one way to get at tigers or leopards, and that is to let them come to you, and not you to go to them. The natives are so lazy, untruthful, and afraid of these animals, that no persuasion will induce them to act as beaters. In vain did we offer, at length, extravagant prices for the beasts. Even fifty dollars, with the bones and carcase thrown in, for each tiger we shot, would not tempt them. The bones and part of the body are greatly prized by the Chinese physicians, as imparting youthful vigour to old or worn-out constitutions. We also offered twenty-five dollars for a shot at a tiger, and ten dollars for the mere sight of one, but equally in vain. Although the people at Pochön strenuously denied[1] the death of any one there from tigers, and even the very existence of these beasts, yet Mr. Campbell, when he visited that village in 1889, was told that in the last year *eighteen* people had been killed by them, and that three tigers, one a confirmed man-eater, infested the district; again, a man-eater was reported in the neighbourhood of the Hu-chih-ryöng,[2] and in the interval between his two visits to that place, the son of the head-man had fallen a victim; and Mr. Campbell told me that from Won-san northwards every third or fourth village had some tale of the ravages of tigers.

But it is only by luck that one comes across these beasts, which by day hide themselves away in the rugged, forest-clad mountains during three-quarters of the year, only appearing in search of food near habitations by night or when the snow has driven their customary prey from the hills. A Russian traveller, coming in the winter from Won-san to Soül, saw a tiger stalking in the snow an old woman in a field, and shot it dead from the high-road. At that season of the year tigers and leopards become very bold. A leopard was seen not long ago in the grounds of the Russian Embassy in Soül, having somehow got over the city wall, and almost every

---

[1] Page 154. [2] Page 188.

winter the city is visited by a similar intruder. The largest tiger-skin I know of measured 14 feet 6 inches from nose to tip of tail, and 8 feet 6 inches from nose to *root of tail* is not uncommon. A good leopard-skin is 9 feet 6 inches from nose to tip of tail, and the thick winter fur of both species is nearly 5 inches thick. I feel sure that if any one could make up his mind to face the hardship and discomfort of a winter in Korea, he would, by living in a well-selected district, obtain good sport with tigers and leopards.

Deer are very numerous, and, with a little trouble, can be readily obtained anywhere away from the large towns. Bears, both brown and black, are not wanting (and could be obtained under the same conditions as tigers), for twenty-eight bear-skins were exported from Won-san in 1890.

Pheasants abound, but require properly trained dogs to put them up, for they are so hawked that it is very difficult to get them to rise without such aid.

As for the wildfowl, they are in millions, and very good sport is to be obtained with them. The only precautions necessary are to dress in white, so as to resemble an ordinary Korean as much as possible, and to have a well-broken dog to retrieve. Even without these, the English fleet at Port Lazareff, averaging ten guns a day, got 1100 head in eight days; while Brazier and Knott in $1\frac{1}{2}$ days got five swan, twenty-eight geese, and four teal; but owing to the disturbing effect of the sailors' sport, they only got one wild duck. On the Anpyön plain there are quantities of wildfowl, but the Japanese go out from Won-san and fire off much powder and shot, with hardly any other effect than to disturb the birds and spoil sport for better shots.

I append a list of some of the furred and feathered inhabitants of Korea. Those marked with an asterisk I have either seen the skins of, or else in their natural state.

*Tiger . . .	Royal, or *Felis tigris*.	Fox.
* ,, . . .	Chinese, the Louchu or Lauhu.	Weasel.
		Marten.
*Leopard . .	The Maou, *F. Chinensis*.	*Otter.
,, . .	The Bulu, *F. Reevesii*.	Beaver.
,, . .	The Snow-Leopard.	Badger.
*Bear . . .	Brown, *Ursus Collaris* or *Ursus Arctos*.	Sable.
		*Ermine.
,, .	Black.	Squirrel . . Grey.
Lynx . . .	*Felis borealis* (?).	* ,, . . Ordinary yellow.
,, . . .	,, *chalybeata*.	* ,, . . Striped (*Sciurus striatus*).
,, . . .	,, *lynx*.	,, . . Flying (doubtful).
*Deer . . .	Red, *Cervus elephas*.	*Pheasant . Chinese, *Phasis torquatus*.
* ,, . . .	The Muntjac, *C. Reevesii*.	,, . Snow, *Crossoptilon mantchuricum* (in Manchuria?).
* ,, . . .	*Pseudaxis mantchurica* or *C. Mantchuricus*.	
* ,, . . .	Fallow.	,, . Argus (doubtful).
,, . . .	*A. Saiga tartarica*.	,, . Reeves (doubtful).
* ,, . . .	The Ling-yang, *A. hemorhedus caudata*.	*Eagle.
		*Hawks.
,, . . .	The Hoang-yang or Yellow Goat, *Procapra gutturosa* (? Manchuria).	*Heron . . (*Ardea cinerea*).
		*Bittern.
		*Swan . . . Wild.
Argali . .	Ovis Ammon (doubtful).	*Geese . . . ,,
Djiggitai .	Asinus onager (doubtful) (in Mongolia (?).)	*Duck . . . ,, Mallard.
		*Teal . . . Baikal Teal, *Boschas formosa*.
Ibex . . .	Doubtful.	
*Pig . . .	Wild.	* ,, . . Ordinary kind.
*Hare . . .	Blue.	*Ibis . . . Pink (*I. Nippon*).

*Ibis . . (*Sinensis*).
*Crane . (several kinds).
*Stork.
*Cormorant.
Pelican . . (doubtful).
*Quail.
*Snipe.
*Widgeon.
*Hazel grouse (*Tetrao Omasia*).
Capercailzie (in Manchuria).
*Magpie . . Korean (blue), (*Cyanopolius cyanus*).

*Jay . . . (Brandt's).
*Golden oriole.
*Pigeons . . Blue rock.
* „ . . Wood.
*Kingfisher.
Grouse Black (*Tetrao tetrix*), in Manchuria.
*Shrike . . (*L. sphenacerus*).
*Woodpeckers Black.
*Jackdaws.
Bustard . (*Otis Dybowski*).

ITINERARY

ITINERARY

It is impossible to accurately render in English the correct pronunciation of Korean names of places, &c., and more especially so because the natives, in saying the same name, vary it greatly amongst themselves in accent and tone; but as far as I can trust my hearing, the sounds given below are nearly correct, and I have the authority of Mr. Ernest Satow to support me in a great measure.

Isolated vowels are pronounced soft as in Italian, but in combinations of vowels and consonants there are some modifications of this rule.

Thus ö is pronounced like *u* in *sun* . . as Po-chön.
,, ai ,, ,, ⎫
,, ei ,, ,, ⎬ *i* in *like* . ,, So-rai-wön.
  ,, Chyei-in-koan.
,, aik ,, ,, *e* in *peck* . ,, Paik-tu-san.
,, eu ,, ,, *u* in *sung* . ,, Ham-heung.
,, an ,, ,, *an* in Spanish *san* . ,, Nam-san.
,, öng ,, ,, *ung* in *sung* . . ,, Söng-do.
,, rim ,, ,, English *rim* . . ,, Ka-rim.
,, { chh, kh, } are highly aspirated, like match-head, Blinkhoolie, cap-
   { ph, th } head, dust-hole.
,, sö is pronounced as between *soo* and *su*, as Sö-tzu river.

Phyöng-an is pronounced between *p-hyung-yan* and *p-hing-yan*; the sound *kw* is nearly rendered by *ko*, thus *kwan* is nearly *ko-an*.

ITINERARY.

Date	Name of Place	Height of Place above Sea-level	Highest Point attained during March above Sea-level	Temperature at 6 A.M.	Start	Arrival	Distance in Li from last Place	Latitude	Longitude	No. of Houses	Weather
1891. Sept. 5	Soŭl	100	...	...	...	...	...	37° 24'	127° 05'	30,000	Fine
,, 5	Wi-erh-mi	285	290	9 p.m. 68°	9.35 a.m.	3.50 p.m.	60	...	...	15	,,
,, 6	Village by river	...	...	...	8.45 a.m.	1 p.m.	40	...	...	20	,,
,, 6	Chan-go-ra-ni	285	285	9 p.m. 65°	3 p.m.	7 p.m.	32	...	...	8	,,
,, 7	Im-jin River	...	...	...	7.30 a.m.	11.30 a.m.	40	...	...	12	,,
,, 7	Hang-na-do-chéra-noup	450	785	8 p.m. 63°	2 p.m.	6 p.m.	40	...	...	30	,,
,, 8	Phyŏng-yang-hwa	...	...	...	7 a.m.	11 a.m.	45	...	...	20	Rain
,, 8	Phyŏng-yang	1200	1500	8 p.m. 61°	1 p.m.	4 p.m.	17	...	...	120	Dull
,, 8	Tang-na-ri	1450	...	...	4 p.m.	5 p.m.	8	...	...	35	,,
,, 9	Village	...	...	...	7.30 a.m.	11.30 a.m.	40	...	...	9	Fine
,, 9	Tan-ga-ni	1450	2100	8 p.m. 65°	1.30 p.m.	7 p.m.	40	...	...	6	,,
,, 10	An-pyŏn (Little)	1100	1630	8 p.m. 66°	8.50 a.m.	1.15 p.m.	50	...	...	8	,,
,, 11	Nam-san*	300	650	8 p.m. 62°	8.30 a.m.	1.15 p.m.	60	39° 10' 34"	127° 31' 50"	80	,,
,, 12	Wŏn-san*	10	170	...	7.45 a.m.	1 p.m.	50	39° 8'	127° 26'	3000	,,
,, 15	Tŏk-wŏn*	50	...	...	10.20 a.m.	...	15	39° 11'	127° 25'	25	,,
,, 15	Ti-kyŏng	...	...	...	...	...	20	...	...	30	,,
,, 15	Mun-chŏn*	50	150	9 p.m. 57°	...	3.20 p.m.	15	39° 15'	127° 22'	100	,,
, 16	Op-ka-chi-ki	...	...	...	7.15 a.m.	...	10	...	...	12	Hot
,, 16	Sŏ-rai-wŏn	...	...	...	...	...	10	39° 20'	...	30	,,
,, 16	Ko-wŏn*	60	...	...	...	12.20 p.m.	20	39° 25' 14"	127° 18'	200	,,

ITINERARY.

Date	Place								Weather
Sept. 16	Tok-chi River				2.35 p.m.	5			Thunder and rain.
,, 16	Yeung-heung *	75	150	8 p.m. 57°		5.45 p.m.	30	39° 27′	,,
,, 18	Keum-ha-wöu				7.45 a.m.	11 a.m.	25	39° 29′	Rain.
,, 18	Ko-san *	150	600		11 a.m.	12.45 p.m.	15		,,
,, 18	Cho-wön				3.30 p.m.		5		,,
,, 18	Chyöng-phyöng	100	500	8 p.m. 62°		6.40 p.m.	35	39° 45′ 30″	30	Fine.
,, 19	Tang-yé		450		7.50 a.m.	12 p.m.	40		500	,,
,, 19	Ori-chun	200		9 p.m. 60°	12.5 p.m.	2.50 p.m.	30	40° 04′	127° 17′	20	,,
,, 21	Sam-ba-gon				8 a.m.	10.45 a.m.	25		15	Rain.
,, 21	Wöng-bu-ni		600		10.45 a.m.	12 noon	15		20	Fine.
,, 21	Chyöng-na-jöng Pass	2050			2.20 p.m.	3.15 p.m.	12		10	Showery.
,, 21	Chyöng-na-jöng	1300	2050		3.15 p.m.	4 p.m.	13		18	,,
,, 22	Pass in Paik-un-san Mountains	4050		6 a.m. 49°	7.30 a.m.	10 a.m.	20	40° 17′ 30″		Overcast.
,, 22	Kotesu	3750			10 a.m.	11.15 a.m.	15		12	Rain.
,, 22	Saseu	3550			2.10 p.m.	5.30 p.m.	40		25	,,
,, 23	Fut-jen-yé		3600	45°	7.30 a.m.	11 a.m.	32	40° 31′		4	Fine.
,, 23	Sok-chöng	3430			11.30 a.m.	1.30 p.m.	18			15	,,
,, 24	Tjen-o-su	3420		45°	8 a.m.	8.30 a.m.	5	40° 41′		12	Unsettled.
,, 24	Teuk-sil-töng	3350	3550	45°	8.30 a.m.	11.30 a.m.	35			14	,,
,, 25	Village				8.15 a.m.	9 a.m.	5			15	Fine.
,, 25	Chang-jin *	3450	3350	49°	9 a.m.	2.30 p.m.	50	40° 52′		300	Rain.
,, 27	Teuk-sil-töng				11.50 a.m.	5.20 p.m.	55				Cloudy and cold.
,, 28	Tjen-o-su			51°	6.30 a.m.	9.30 a.m.	35			...	,,
,, 28	Memel Ryöng (Pass)	5300			11.30 a.m.	2.30 p.m.	25	40° 35′ 30″	127° 24′		Fine.
,, 28	Sui-tmni	3870		41°	3 p.m.	5.15 p.m.	25			8	,,
,, 29	Ferry				6.15 a.m.	6.45 a.m.	5			5	,,
,, 29	Sorin Ryöng (Pass)	5770			7.10 a.m.	10 a.m.	27	40° 38′ 30″	127° 26′		,,
,, 29	Tong-kol-at	4870			10.15 a.m.	1 p.m.	35			10	,,
,, 29	Sesidong	4140			3 p.m.	7.25 p.m.	45	40° 41′	127° 37′	34	,,

ITINERARY.

Date	Name of Place.	Height of Place above Sea-level.	Highest Point attained during March.	Temperature at 6 A.M.	Hour of Start.	Hour of Arrival.	Distance in Li from last Place.	Latitude.	Longitude.	No. of Houses.	Weather.
1891. Sept. 30	Yangari	3840	...	34°	8.30 a.m.	12.30 p.m.	35	40° 45′	127° 44′	30	Fine.
,, 30	Neun-gwi *	3490	4640	...	3 p.m.	5.30 p.m.	25	40° 46′	127° 51′	15	,,
Oct. 1	Ho-rin-cham *	3300	4090	31°	7.10 a.m.	9.15 a.m.	20	...	...	20	,,
,, 1	Kapsan *	3040	...	...	9.45 a.m.	2.50 p.m.	45	40° 56′ 9″	...	120	,,
,, 2	Toug-in *	3050	3550	37°	2.35 p.m.	5.55 p.m.	40	41° 3′ 25″	...	50	,,
,, 3	Sun-yun-i	3150	...	35°	7.10 a.m.	7.50 a.m.	5	...	...	15	,,
,, 3	An-kang Ryŏng (Pass)	4250	...	...	7.50 a.m.	8.20 a.m.	6	...	...	6	,,
,, 3	An-kang-poi *	...	...	...	8.30 a.m.	8.50 a.m.	1	...	...	10	,,
,, 3	Un-chong *	3050	4650	29°	8.50 a.m.	11 a.m.	25	41° 12′	127° 54′	100	,,
,, 3	Po-chŏn *	2950	...	...	2.30 p.m.	9.30 p.m.	63	41° 22′ 30″	127° 49′	12	,,
,, 5	Ka-rim	2850	...	...	9.30 a.m.	11 a.m.	15	...	...	6	,,
,, 5	Po-chŏn	...	3950	40°	12 noon	1.45 p.m.	12	...	...	...	Rain.
,, 6	Un-chong	...	...	...	8.40 a.m.	2.20 p.m.	45	...	...	...	Fine.
,, 6	Sun-yun-i	...	...	55°	4.20 p.m.	8 p.m.	32	...	...	...	Cold wind.
,, 7	Kap-san	...	...	...	7.30 p.m.	11.5 a.m.	45	...	...	...	,,
,, 7	Ho-rin-cham	...	...	31°	1.20 p.m.	5.30 p.m.	45	...	...	...	,,
,, 8	Neun-gwi	3490	...	...	6 a.m.	8.40 a.m.	20	40° 41′	127° 57′	30	,,
,, 8	Pass	4600	...	...	9.40 a.m.	12.30 p.m.	22	40° 37′ 30″	127° 58′ 30″	...	,,
,, 8	Chan-ka-cham *	4060	5050	...	12.30 p.m.	2.30 p.m.	20	40° 32′	127° 57′ 30″	10	,,
,, 8	Houng-so-wŏn *	4200	...	24°	4.20 p.m.	8.35 p.m.	40	...	...	8	Fine.
,, 9	Hu-chih Ryŏng (Pass)	4550	...	...	7 a.m.	10.40 a.m.	40	40° 28′	128° 2′ 30″	...	,,
,, 9	Chyei-in-koan *	2000	...	...	10.55 a.m.	2.10 p.m.	35	40° 23′	128° 10′ 30″	12	,,
,, 9	Si-go-ri	1000	...	...	4.10 p.m.	5.30 p.m.	15	...	...	15	,,
,, 9	Chang-heung *	600	...	44°	5.30 p.m.	7.30 p.m.	5	40° 18′	128° 16′	85	,,
,, 10	Noyada	...	...	...	6.30 a.m.	9.30 p.m.	38	...	...	50	,,
,, 10	Chŏng-mo-ru	...	...	...	9.30 a.m.	10 a.m.	3	...	...	50	,,
,, 10	Puk-chhŏng	100	...	...	10 a.m.	10.15 a.m.	4	40° 10′	128° 17′	1200	,,

ITINERARY.

Date	Place								Fine.
Oct. 10	To-chih Ryöng (Pass)	580	...	1.30 p.m.	4 p.m.	25	...	128° 10′	...	,,
,, 10	Pyöng-po-ri	...	...	4 p.m.	7 p.m.	25	40° 05′	128° 3′	30	,,
,, 11	Choll-nam	...	51°	6.50 a.m.	9.30 a.m.	30	39° 59′	127° 57′	50	,,
,, 11	Houng-wŏn *	50	...	9.30 a.m.	10.50 a.m.	15	39° 58′	127° 52′	180	,,
,, 11	Haamheung-cha'im *	...	...	12.30 p.m.	3 p.m.	20	39° 56′ 30″	127° 49′ 30″	19	,,
,, 11	Hang-kal Ryöng (Pass)	1120	...	4 p.m.	5.20 p.m.	15	...	...	...	,,
,, 11	Tong-sa-mi	...	...	5.20 p.m.	5.50 p.m.	5	...	...	20	,,
,, 12	Tong-sang-kuan *	...	51°	6.15 a.m.	8.50 a.m.	25	39° 54′	127° 41′	30	,,
,, 12	Ham-heung *	...	55°	9.50 a.m.	12.15 p.m.	30	39° 51′ 25″	127° 35′	†6000	,,
,, 13	Chyöng-phyöng	...	...	12 noon	4 p.m.	50	...	...	...	,,
,, 13	Cho-wön	...	51°	6.30 p.m.	10 p.m.	35	...	...	...	,,
,, 14	Yeung-heung	...	...	6.45 a.m.	10 a.m.	45	...	...	...	,,
,, 14	So-rai-wön	...	...	1 p.m.	4.30 p.m.	55	...	...	...	,,
,, 14	Mun-chön	...	...	7.45 p.m.	11 p.m.	25	...	...	...	,,
,, 15	Wön-san	...	52°	8 a.m.	11.40 a.m.	50	...	...	...	,,
						†2495				

* Posting-station.   † 11 li equal 3 miles about.

Altitudes were taken with an aneroid graduated to 9000 feet, and it showed the altitude of Teuk-sil-töng to be identically the same on September 24 and 27, so its performances must have been at least constant, if not tolerably accurate. The general map of Korea is taken from the Royal Geographical Society's map, with a few alterations and additions by myself; the route map is taken from the Russian Staff Map, which is based on the Japanese official one, with alterations and additions according to my observation.

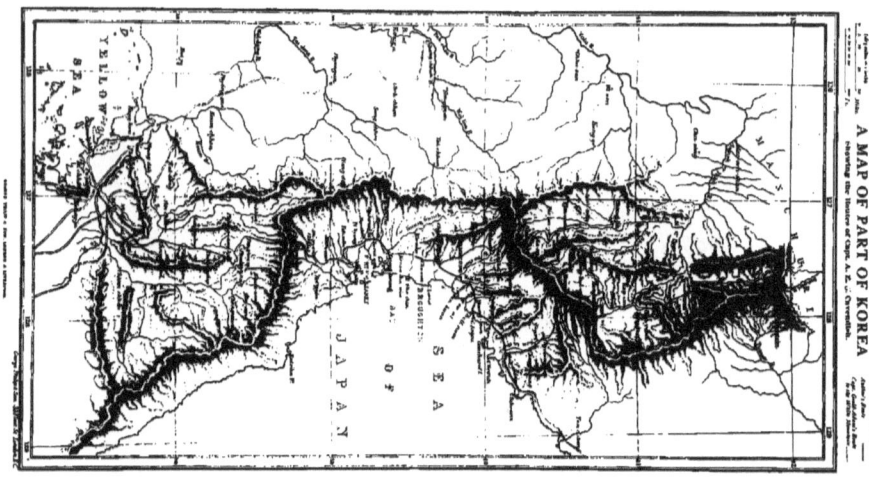

INDEX

A

ADDER, brown, 64, 137 ; narrow escape from, 157
Advisers to the King, 44
Ah Sin, Mr., of Won-san, 89
Alphabet, Korean, little use of, 155
Amber beads, 94 ; mouthpiece to pipes, 94
Amnok or Yalu river, 101, 135, 153, 159–161, 169
An-kang-poi village, 185
An-kang-ryöng (pass), 145
An-pyön monastery, 74 ; camp at village, 77
—— plain, 78
—— —— tigers and leopards on, 77, 97 ; wildfowl on, 205
Archers, 43, 106, 192
Arms, native, 43
Army of Phyöng-an, 42
Ash, mountain, 121
Attendants, official, 15, 95, 143
Azaleas, 121, 173

B

BAGGAGE, our own, 31 ; weight of, 51, 101 ; left at Kapsan, 145, 185 ; the cook's, 29 ; weight of, 145
Barley, cultivation of, 134, 138 ; trade in, 48
Bathing at Chefoo, 12 ; on the road, 58, 62, 74
Battlefield of 1592, 80
Beans, cultivation of, 20, 54, 66, 191 ; trade in, 48

Bears, black, 131, 154, 204, 205 ; brown, 205
Bear-skins, export of, 204
Bearers, difficulty in getting, 151, 158 ; behaviour of, 166, 168 ; good-nature of, 169, 179
Beaver, 165, 205
Beaver-skins, tribute in, 81
Bees, cultivation of, 69
Beech-trees, 115, 121 ; large, 116, 133
Bell, great, at Soŭl, 22
Bellington, Mr., on the Tientsin Railway, 12
Birch-trees, 116, 121, 133, 173
Bird-traps, 119
Biscuit, weevilly, 89, 163
Bones, cow, export of, 35 ; tiger, as Chinese medicine, 202
Boundaries of provinces, 69, 116, 155, 177
Brazier, Mr., his hospitality, 94, 102 ; he meets a leopard, 99
Bridges, at An-pyön, 74 ; at Chang-jin, 123 ; at Ham-heung, 198 ; at Teuk-sil-töng, 124 ; stored away in summer, 81, 103 ; usual construction, 81
British Consulate-General, 30
—— trade with Korea, 47
Bulls, loads for, 34 ; price of, 34 ; size of, 34
Bu-si-ka-chi river, 191
Bustard, 206

C

CABBAGE, cultivation of, 54
Calling on Mandarins, 86, 225, 194

INDEX

Campbell, Mr., his difficulty with Kapsan people, 110
Camping in graveyard, 55, 61, 109; on threshing-floor, 71, 134
—— not safe on account of tigers, 67, 71, 134
Card, mine rejected, 196
Cards, our visiting, 30
Carts, description of, 112
Cash, copper, debased, 97; preferred to silver, 60; rate of exchange for, 93, 97, 130; weight of, 145
Castor-oil plants, cultivation of, 20, 53
Cattle, price of, 34; size of, 34; trade in, 35, 148, 158, 166
Chang-gé, road to, 125, 129
Chang-heung, 189
Chang-jin, bridges at, 124; camp at, 127; country about, 225; curiosity of inhabitants, 127; deer-drive at, 128; estimated distance to, 96; real distance to, 126
—— Prefect of, civility of, 127; his lying causes us delay, 130; exchanges presents, 126
—— river, salmon in, 130; scenery of its valley, 119; source of, 117, 121; tributary of, 121, 123
Changorani, camp at, 61
Chang-pai mountains, 160, 165, 169
Chanka-cham, change ponies at, 187
Chefoo, coolies at, 11; exports of, 12; fortification and garrison of, 12
Chémulpho, description of, 16
Cherry-trees, wild, 121
Chickens, difficulty in procuring, 114; German travellers shooting, 115
Children, handsome, 83; method of carrying, 79; weaning of, deferred, 59
Chillies, cultivation of, 54
China, tribute paid to, 80
Chinese bandits, 148; characters, use of, 155
—— influence in Korea, 37, 90; population in, 49

Chinese traders, rescued by Capt. Devenish, 13; Resident at Soŭl, 28; his police, 28, 91; Consul at Won-san, 90; his geese, 99; his police, 91
Chinamen, ruffianly, at Un-chong, 146; at Po-chön, 150; in Yalu basin, 160, 172
Cholera at Won-san, 88; mortality from, at Fu-san, 88
Chollnam village, 191
Chöng-mo-ru village, 190
Cho-wön, halt at, 199
Chyei-in-koan village, 188
Chyöng-na-jöng village and pass, 115
Chyöng-phyöng, 109, 199
Clothing, native, 19, 27, 54, 94, 132, 159, 180, 189
College, cadet, 45; royal, mismanagement of, 26
Consulate-General, British new, 30
Cook, our, age of, 67; baggage of, 29, 145; difficulty caused by him as interpreter, 186, 193; embezzlements of, 156, 182; gets drunk, 186; linguistic attainments of, 20; troubles of, 28, 66, 70, 186
Coolies, naked, 11, 16; load of, 36; pack-frame of, 35
Cotton, cultivation of, 54
Cow frightened of us, 145
Crab-apple tree, 121
Cranes, 66, 81, 106, 113, 194, 206
Creepers, 75, 193
Cultivation, 20, 53, 55
Curfew regulations, 22
Curiosity of natives, 61, 63, 106, 109, 127, 137, 141, 147, 185
Curious geological formation, 80
Currency of Korea, 95
Customs, administered by Chinese, 25, 37; revenue from, 26, 47

D

Deer, 78, 122, 154, 175, 204, 205
—— drive at Chang-jin, 128; fence, 152

INDEX 217

Delay, from inability to get ponies, 131;
  by officials, 129, 195; by rain, 29, 106,
  109, 113, 118; by servants, 57, 136; by
  stranding of steam-launch, 17; on the
  road, 76
Devenish, Capt., his kindness to wrecked
  Chinese traders, 13
Dialects of Korean, 154
Disease, 27, 78, 83, 196
Donkey as beast of burden, 34
Donnelly, Mr., his kindness to us, 12
Dogs, hatred of white men, 188
Dragon-flies, 122
Duck, wild, 118, 132, 138, 181, 194, 200,
  205
Duty, military, of hunters, 43; of
  officers, 46; of soldiers, 15, 45
Dye, General, military adviser to king, 44

E

ESCAPE from snake-bite, 157; from
  broken leg, 193
Etiquette, equestrian, 33; social, 95,
  107, 127
Examination requisite for holding office,
  41
Exchange, rate of, for cash, at Chang-jin,
  130; at Kap-san, 141, 145; at Soŭl, 97;
  at Won-san, 95

F

FALCONS as tribute, 80
Fallow-deer, 122, 152, 205
Fern, maiden-hair, 183
Ferry, 59, 82, 107, 118, 132, 140
—— boats, 60, 122, 135
Fertility of country, 20
Fir-trees, Scotch, 116, 121, 193
Fires in forests, 133, 135, 149, 165
Firewood, destruction of trees for, 56
Fish, trade in, 47; trout, 57, 122, 179;
  salmon, 104, 130; herring, 48; whale, 48
Fish, spearing, 103
Fishing tackle, primitive, 119, 179

Flax, 54
Fleas, 71, 74, 137, 141, 145, 200
Flies, ferocious, 66
Food of natives, 33, 48, 52, 155, 163,
  195
Foreign adviser to King, 44
—— Affairs, Minister for, 29
—— population, 49
Forests, destruction of, 133, 135, 165
Frontier posts, 150
Fruit, cultivation of, 54, 74
Funeral, customs, 56, 192; of Japanese
  Envoy, 45; of Queen Dowager, 45
Furniture of houses, 150
Fu-san, mortality from cholera at, 88;
  foreign population of, 49
Fnt-jen-yé, ferry at, 118

G

GAME, difficulty in finding, 67, 78, 122,
  202
—— of Korea, 205
Garden, the Queen's, 30
Garrison of Chefoo, 12; of Soŭl, 44
Gate of Soŭl, 21, 52
Geese, Mr. Woo's, carried off by tiger, 99
—— wild, 138, 194, 200, 181, 205
Gen-san, see Won-san
Geological formation, curious, 80
German travellers, delayed by rain, 79;
  engraving their names in sacred places,
  201; shooting chickens, 115
Glacial action, traces of, 103
Gold, tribute in, to China, 80; export
  of, 108
—— washings, 108, 109, 146
Goold-Adams, Capt., bitten by flies, 63;
  starts for the White Mountain, 155;
  parts from me in Manchuria, 156; his
  ascent of White Mountain, 158-181
Governor of Hamgyong province, call
  on, 197
Graphite, outcrop of, 108

Graveyard, camping in, 55, 61, 109; carefully kept, 55, 80, 144, 192; on sea-shore, 191
Grosvenor, Mr., his rate of hiring transport, 93
Grouse, black, 206; hazel, 162, 206
Guild of Chinese traders present tablet to Capt. Devenish, 14; in Manchuria, 165
Guns, native, 128

H

HAIR, method of wearing, 143
Hamgyong, call on governor of province of, 197
Ham-heung, 109; bridge, 198; delay at, 195; description of, 198; Mandarius of, 194; rudeness of people at, 196; silverwork of, 146
—— Prefect of, rudeness of, 197; he sends money to repay me, 198
—— chain, village, 192
Han, river, fortifications along, 17 journey up, 17–20
—— valley, fertility of, 53; scenery of, 54
Hands, small, a beauty, 84; care bestowed on, by Mandarins, 84
Hangnadou-ché-ra-noup, camp at, 63
Hang-kal-ryöng (pass), 193
Hang-pai-do, landing at, 20
Han-yang, see Soŭl
Hats of Mandarins, 94, 194; cost of, 27
Hawking, 147, 204
Hazel grouse, 162, 206
Hemp, cultivation of, 53
Hillier, Mr., British Consul-General, his kindness to us, 21, 28, 31, 52; his garden, 30; his house, 21; photographs us, 51
Hintze, Mr., kindly advances money, 95
Hire of ponies, 31, 97
Hives, description of, 69
Ho-chön river, 136, 139, 145
Hoiyang river, 65

Honey, 70, 113, 130
Horincham village, 139, 186
Hospital, American, 26; mismanagement of Royal, 26
Houng-so-wön, 187
Houng-wön village, 191
House, description of a Korean, 76, 137; roofs of birch-bark, 117, 188
Ho-wön village, 191
Hu-chih-ryöng (pass) and village, 188
—— tiger at, 203
Hunter, civility of, at Teuk-sil-töng, 122, 131; military duties of, 43

I

IBIS, pink, 106, 194, 205
Idlers, numbers of, 41
Ignorance concerning distances, 96
Im-jin river, 59, 63; tributary of, 58
In-chhön, see Chémulpho, Prefect of, 15
Insect life, bugs and fleas, 71, 74, 137, 141, 145, 200; dragon-flies, 122; flies, 63; mosquitoes, 57, 109
Interpreter, our, 28; failings of, 175
Ironstone near Kap-san, 140
Irrigation of rice-fields, 55
Itinerary, 209

J

JAPAN, tribute paid to, 80; use of Chinese characters in, 155
Japanese, attempt to evade treaty, 91; bullying of natives, 18; civility of junk-coolies, 19; Consul at Won-san, 90; fishermen, 48; forced to leave Soŭl, 91; influence in Korea, 37, 90
—— invasions, 17, 37, 80; population, 49; post-office, 37; steam-launch, 16
Japanese Envoy at Soŭl and his police, 91; funeral of, 45
Jays, 122, 206
Jenchuan, see Chémulpho
Jinsen, see Chémulpho

INDEX   219

Jones, "Brother," 16, 21
Junk, night spent on Japanese, 19; attempt to use Korean, 17; wreck of Chinese, 13

K

KANG, description of, 78; warmth from, 118
Kaoliang, cultivation of, 54
Kap-san, boundary of district, 135, 155; danger of Mr. Campbell in, 110; mineral resources of, 142; Prefect of, 142, 185; stay at, 141, 185
Karim village, 155, 160
Kerr, Mr., Vice-Consul, his kindness to us, 15
Keum-ha-wön gold-washings, 108
Khota river, 194
King of Korea, despotism of, 25; enforced fidelity to marriage vows, 25; extravagance of, 25, 26; titles of, 24
Kingfishers, 113, 122
Kirin, 175
Korea, army of, 37; curfew regulations of, 22; currency of, 97; corruption in internal affairs of, 40, 46,; danger from Russia, 38; invaded by Japanese, 17, 37, 80; King of, 24; navy of, 38; political situation of, 37; population of, 40, 49; trade of, 47; tribute paid to China and Japan by, 80, 81; use of Chinese characters in, 155
Korean alphabet only used by coolies and women, 155
——— language, ceremonial changes in, 186
——— ——— dialects of, 154
——— women, dress of, 82, 132; disfiguring sores of, 82, 196; hard work of, 83; points of beauty of, 83; ugliness of, 83, 125; crossing path unlucky, 125
Koreans, characteristics of, 46, 180; civility of, 74; curiosity of, 61, 63, 106, 109, 127, 137, 141, 147, 185; diseases of, 27, 78, 83, 196; economical habits of, 20, 82; filthy manners of, 17, 27, 137; food of, 33, 48, 52, 155, 163, 195; houses of, 76; immorality of, 83; laziness of, 47, 84; lying of, 20, 115, 176, 195; pedestrian powers of, 31, 36, 45; rudeness of, 190–196; superstitions of, 63, 133, 154, 156, 163, 167, 172
Ko-san, halt at, 109
Kot-e-su, halt at, 117
Ko-wön, halt at, 105
Kut-yang, village of, 113

L

LANDSLIPS, 170
Laporte, Mr., customs officer, 15
Larch-trees, 160, 173
Lava, deposits of, 152; plains of, 62, 68, 76, 187
Laziness of natives, 47, 84
Legendre, General, foreign adviser to King, 44
Leopards, fresh track of, 78; infesting mountains, 71; at Won-san, 97; in Soul, 202; on An-pyön plain, 97, skins of, used by Mandarins, 127, 141; size of, 204; export of, 98,
Letter, Foreign Office, 29, 127
——— pony, 104; forgery by servants, 104, 180
Li, length of, 96
——— posts, 59, 155, 176
Loan, efforts to raise American, 44
Localities, difficulty in ascertaining names of, 68
Lynx, 205

M

MAIDENHAIR fern, 183
Maize, cultivation of, 20
Manchuria, parting with G.-A. in, 156; settlers in, 153, 165, 172; trade with, 153, 166
Maple-trees, 73, 116, 121
Maps, inaccuracy of, 96
Mapus, dawdling of, 58, 75, 135, 199;

defection of, 110; knowledge of country, 15, 68; payment of, 97, 126, 145; sickness of, 123; stupidity of, 77; take wrong road, 55
Mapuh, river port of Soŭl, 20
Market-days, 85
Marriage procession, 132
Medical treatment, our, 123
Memel-ryŏng (pass), 132
Military adviser, 44; arms, 43; system, 40; training, 42, 45
Mills, water, description of, 75; in use, 120
—— paper, 48
—— rice, 49
Millet, cultivation of, 20, 54, 66; as food, 54, 163
Min family, 43, 93
Min-yuen-ik, Prince, at Hong-Kong, 30, 91; nearly murdered, 91
Min-yuen-shao, Prince, 29
Mismanagement of Government institutions, 26
Mole-skins, blue, as tribute, 81
Monasteries, Buddhist, 71, 77, 201
Money, difficulty in getting, 95, 130, 141
Monk devoured by tiger, 71
Mosquitoes, 57, 109
Moss, stag's-horn, 133
Mountains, height of, 119
Mun-chŏn, camp at, 103; late arrival at, 199
Muntjac, the, 205; Brazier's pet, 88

N

NAM-SAN, halt at, 76
Nam-ta-cheni river, 188
Nature, Korean admiration of, 31
—— worship, 63, 133, 154, 156, 163, 184, 167, 172
Naval affairs, how administered, 42
Neun-gwi, halt at, 139, 186
Nienstead, Lieut.-Col., drill instructor, 37, 44; his rapid promotion, 21

Non-commissioned officers, promotion of, 45
Noyada village, 190

O

OAK-TREES, 116, 193
Oats, cultivation of, 117, 134, 138; export of, 148
Officers, military duties of, 45
—— non-commissioned, 45
Official attendants, 15, 95, 143
—— etiquette, 33, 95, 107, 127
Officials, corrupt practices of, 25, 26, 44; lying of, 131, 195; punishment of, 46; travelling, 16, 107, 114
Oiesen, Mr., his hospitality, 85, 200; his house, 87
Orichun, delayed by rain at, 112
Otter, 205

P

PACK-SADDLE, 51
—— frame of coolies, 35
Paik-tu-san, see White Mountain
Paik-un mountains, crossing, 116, 188
Palace, new, at Soŭl, 22
Pamum-ryŏng (pass), 191
Paper, Korean trade in, 48; tribute in, 80
—— mill, 48
Pass in mountains, Ankang-ryŏng, 145; Hangkal-ryŏng, 193; Huchih-ryŏng, 188; in Paik-un-san mountains, 116; Memel-ryong, 132; near Houngso-wŏn; 187; near Neungwi, 186; Sorin-ryŏng, 135; Pamum-ryŏng, 191
Passports, 30
Peach-trees, 54, 74
Pearls, tribute in, 80
Pears, Chefoo, 11; Korean, 54, 74, 199
Pedestrian powers of Koreans, 31, 36, 45
Persimmon-trees, 54
Pheasants, 66, 77, 130, 154, 181, 204, 205
—— hawking of, 147, 204

INDEX

Photographs by Mr. Hillier, 51 ; failure of our own, 156
Phyöng-an, province of, 116 ; army of, 42, 45
Phyöng-yang, 66
Pigeons, blue rock, 138, 206 ; wood, 57 62, 132, 206
Pigs, bait for tiger, 99 ; wild, 122, 175, 205
Pine-trees, 61, 115, 133
Pipes, tobacco, 14, 82
Plum-trees, wild, 121
Po-chön, 150, 158, 178 ; packages left at, 178 ; man-eating tiger at, 158
Ponies, bad temper of, 33, 113, 193 ; cost of hiring, 31, 93, 198 ; description of, 33, 51 ; difficulties in hiring, 33, 93, 97 ; food of, 33 ; galls of, 97 ; loads of, 33, 101 ; pack-saddle for, 51 ; price of, 34 ; shoeing of, 120 ; sureness of foot of, 33, 52, 70, 131
Pony, a blind, 70
Pony-letter, 104 ; forgery of, by servants 104, 180
Pony-men, see Mapu
Poplar-trees, large, 132, 140
Population of Korea, 40, 49 ; of Soül, 23 ; of Won-san, 49, 90 ; foreign, 49
Port Lazareff, British fleet in, 200
Posting system, 86, 104
Post-office under Japanese, 37, 90
Post-ponies, difficulty in getting, 195 ; employment of, by us, 105, 131, 179, 185, 187 ; speed of, 189, 194 ; wretched condition of, 189
Potatoes, cultivation of, 134, 138, 172
Prefect of Chang-jin, civility of, 127 ; delays us by lying, 130 ; exchange of presents with, 126, 130
—— of Ham-heung, his rudeness, 197; sends money to repay me, 198
—— of Inchhön, 15
—— of Kap-san, 141, 185 ; his salary, 143
—— of Tök-wön, 86, 95 ; deceived by our servants, 104, 180

Prefects, number of, 40
Provinces, boundaries between, 69, 116, 177
Puk-chöng, prefecture of, 190 ; rudeness of people at, 190
Pumice-stone, 152 ; causes white appearance of White Mountain, 153, 173
Pyöng-po-ri, halt at, 191

Q

Quail, 181, 206
Queen of Korea, her garden, 31 ; influence in the state of, 25
—— Dowager, funeral of, 45

R

Railway, Tientsin, Chinese ideas concerning, 12
—— Trans-Siberian, 38
Rain, delays us, 29, 106, 109, 113
Raspberries, wild, 75
Red-deer, 205
Revolution in Soül, 91
Rice, cultivation of, 20, 53, 66, 81, 191 ; to propitiate evil spirits, 156, 163, 167 ; tribute in, 80 ; trade in, 47
Rice-fields, irrigation of, 55, 103, 194
—— mills, 49
Rivers, Amnok or Yalu, 101, 135, 153, 159 ; Bu-si-ka-chi, 191 ; Chang-jin, 117; Han, 17, 53 ; Hoiyang, 65 ; Ho-chhön, 136 ; Im-jin, 59, 63 ; Khota, 194 ; Nam-ta-che-ni, 188; Sha-phyöng, 135; Shé-chön, 109 ; Shika, 191 ; So-chön, 197, 112 ; Sungari, 169, 184 ; Tök-chi, 105 ; Tumen, 184 ; Yeung-heung, 106, 199
Roads, description of, 72; forest, 133, 164; good, 103, 115 ; infamous, 72, 117
Rosemary, wild, 75
Russia, danger to Korea from, 38
Russian embassy at Soül, 16, 200; envoy, 16

S.

SABLE, 165, 205
Salmon, 104, 130
Sambagon, village, 115
Samshu at Un-chong, 146; cook gets drunk on, 186
Sam-su, 71, 126, 155
Sanitation, want of, 21, 22, 24, 47, 62
Saseu, stay at, 118
Scenery, beauty of, 73, 116, 117; native admiration of, 31; of Chang-jin river, 119; of Han river, 17, 53; of Im-jin river, 63; of Paik-un mountains, 116; of White Mountain, 174, 183
Scott, Mr., Vice-Consul, a Korean scholar, 21; helps us to get ponies, 21; takes servants back to Shanghai, 28
Seal-bearers, 40, 94
Serpents, reverence for, 138
Servants, 11, 28, dilatoriness of, 57; forgery by, 104, 180
Sesidong, extent of cultivation at, 138; rough quarters at, 137
Shanghai Club, 11
Shantung dialect, 161
Sha-phyöng river, 135
Shé-chön river, 109
Shika river, 191
Shoeing pony, 120
Siberian Railway, escape of convict labourers on, 100; mismanagement of, 39
Sigori village, 189
Silk, tribute to China in, 80
Silver, inappreciation of, 60; native work in, 146; shoe or sycee, 102, 144; tribute to China in, 80
Slate formation, 145, 147
Sleds, use of, 34, 139, 145
Snakes, 64, 105; poisonous adder, 137; narrow escape from, 157
Snipe, 81, 113, 206
Snow, 177
So-chön river, 197, 112

Sok-chung, camp at, 119
Soldier driven away by servants, 144, 176; given as guide, 22, 95, 144, 185, 191
Soldiers as official attendants, 15, 42; number of, 40; value in military sense, 46
So-rai-wön, delay at, 199
So-rin-ryöng (pass), 135
Soŭl, attractions of, 24; British Consulate-General at, 30; gates of, 21, 52; palace of King at, 22; population of, 23; revolution in, 91; Russian Embassy, 16, 203; streets of, 22, 52; walls of, 21, 52; great bell of, 22; leopards in, 203
Spearing fish, 103
Spectacles worn by officials, 95
Squirrels, 116, 133, 205
Stag's-horn moss, 133
Steamers, Japanese mail, 16, 90; Korean, 42
Steward, Mr., a Chinaman, 15
Storks, 81, 206
Stranded on sandbank, 17
Strawberries, 30; poisonous (?), 65
Streets of Soŭl, 22, 52
Stripling, Mr., his position in Korea, 29; lends us his boy Yeung, 29
Sul-mul, camp at, 134
Sungari river, 169, 184
Sun-yun-i village, 185
Superintendent of trade at Chémulpho, 15
—— at Won-san, 86
Susu, clothes made from, 54; cultivation of, 20, 54
Sycamore-trees, 121, 193
Sycee or silver ingot, 102, 144
System, military, 40; posting, 86
Swans, wild, 204, 205

T.

TAN-GA-NI, camp at, 70
Tang-na-ri, camp at, 66

INDEX

Tang-yé village, 111
Teal, flight of, 109; common, 138, 200, 205
—— blue-winged or Baikal, 114, 205
Telegraph line, Soŭl to Won-san, 55, 84, 92
—— Won-san to Wladivostock, 92
Temperature, 27, 57 ; *see* Itinerary
Tent, our, curiosity excited by, 61, 127;
 description of, 32 ; left at Kap-san, 145
Threshing-floor of village, 71, 134
Tide, rise and fall of, at Chémulpho, 16 ;
 on east coast, 191
Tientsin Railway, Chinese ideas about, 12
Tigers, alive, 97 ; at Won-san, 99 ; devouring monk, 71 ; danger feared to us from, 32, 71, 134 ; infesting mountains, 67, 74, 154 ; at Po-chön, 158 ; reported presence of, 128, 154 ; native fear of, 77, 100, 128, 148, 205 ; at Huchih-ryöng, 203
Tiger-guns, 128
—— traps, 99, 144
—— skins, export of, 98 ; size of, 204 ;
 tribute in, 81
Tjen-ö-su village, 119, 132
Tobacco, coarseness of, 94 ; cultivation of, 20, 66, 134, 191 ; size of plant, 53
Tok-chi river, 105
Tök-wön, Prefect of, his civility, 86, 95 ;
 his yamen, 102
Tong-in, halt at, 144
Tong-kol-at, halt at, 136
Tong-sa-mi village, disturbance at, 193
Tong-sang-kuan, good ponies from, 194
Torches, cause of forest fires, 149, 183 ;
 travelling with, for fear of wild beasts, 136, 149
Trade, statistics of, 47, 48 ; in cattle, 34, 148, 158, 166 ; in bear-skins, 204 ; in cow-bones, 35 ; in hides, 35 ; in leopard and tiger skins, 98
—— Superintendent of, at Chémulpho 15 ; at Won-san, 86
Training, military, 42, 45
Trans-Siberian Railway, 38
Traps for birds, 120 ; for tigers, 99

Trappers, Korean, 160, 165, 167, 170
Treaty, Korean, with China and Japan, 91
Trees, destruction for firewood of, 56, 64,
Tribute paid to China and Japan, 80
Trollope, Rev. Mr., devotion to missionary work, 37 ; visits Buddhist monasteries and Won-san, 201
Trout, 57, 122, 132, 179
Tumen river, 184

U.

UN-CHONG, Chinamen at, 146 ; gold at, 146 ; head-man of, 146 ; stay at, 146, 185

V.

VEGETABLES in foreign gardens, 102 ;
 native, 54, 77, 134, 138
Virginia creeper, 193
Volcanic action, signs of, 62, 64, 67, 76, 140, 153
Volcano, extinct, *see* White Mountain
Voluntary service of army, 39, 44

W.

WALNUT-TREES, 115, 119, 127
War, Board of, 42
Washing, of clothes, 27 ; our difficulties in, 62, 74, 122 ; native aversion to, 24, 27, 123
Water-mills, description of, 75 ; in use, 120
—— Japanese, 75, 120
Weaning of children, deferred, 59
Whale-fishing, 48
Wheat, trade in, 48
Whisky, Korean appreciation of, 127, 142, 192 ; loss of, 62, 199
White Mountain, 102 ; height of, 152, 173 ;
 Goold-Adams starts for, 155 ; native legends concerning, 153, 156, 184 ; no snow on, 153, 157 ; royal sacrifice to spirits of, 184 ; view of, 152, 157, 183 ;

ascent of, 158-181 ; lake on summit of, 174
Widgeon, 106, 132, 200, 206
Wi-erh-mi, camp at, 53
Wildfowl, numbers near Won-san, 181, 202, 204
Willow-trees, 121, 140 ; home of jays, 122
Wladivostock, closed by ice, 38 ; Korean trader journeying to, 111 ; railway work in, 39 ; reign of terror in, 100 ; trade in cattle and oats to, 35, 148, 158
Wöng-bo-ni, halt at, 115
Won-san, coveted by Russia, 38 ; foreign population of, 49 ; foreign settlement at, 85, 89 ; my return to, 200 ; tales of the cholera at, 88 ; tigers and leopards at, 99 ; wildfowl near, 181, 200, 204 ; population of native town, 85 ; trade of, 48, 89, 97, 203

Woo, Mr., Chinese Consul at Won-san, 90 ; his geese carried off by tiger, 99 ; lends us a sycee, 102
Wylde, Dr., his devotion to medicine, 26

Y.

YALU river, see Amnok
Yangari, village, 138
Yeung, our boy, 29 ; farewell letter to his wife, 154 ; chastisement of, 176 ; misconduct of, 180
Yeung-heung, camp at, 106, 107 ; halt at, 199 ; gold-washings, 108 ; river, 106, 199
Yuan, Chinese Resident at Soŭl, 28, 91 ; his police force, 91
Yuen-san, see Won-san

THE END.

www.ingramcontent.com/pod-product-compliance
Lightning Source LLC
Chambersburg PA
CBHW032106230426

43672CB00009B/1652